Notes from the Night

Broadway Books
New York

# Notes
# from the
# Night

*A Life After Dark*

TAYLOR PLIMPTON

Published in the United States by Broadway Books, an imprint of the
Crown Publishing Group, a division of Random House, Inc., New York.

www.crownpublishing.com

BROADWAY BOOKS and the Broadway Books colophon are trademarks of
Random House, Inc.

Library of Congress Cataloging-in-Publication Data
Plimpton, Taylor,
Notes from the night : a life after dark / Taylor Plimpton.—1st ed.
1. Plimpton, Taylor, 1976—Homes and haunts—New York (State)—New
York. 2. Nightlife—New York (State)—New York. 3. New York (N.Y.)—
Social life and customs. I. Title.
F128.57.P58A3 2010
974.7'1—dc22                    2010009476

ISBN 978-0-307-71622-4

PRINTED IN THE UNITED STATES OF AMERICA

Design by Elizabeth Rendfleisch

10  9  8  7  6  5  4  3  2  1

First Edition

For Dad, who was never convinced there was anything inherently wrong in having fun . . .

## Author's Note

This is a memoir, and the story that follows is entirely true. Nonetheless, in attempting to capture the reality of an evening out, I have taken certain liberties: The one night described in this book is actually a composite of several nights; I have also altered the names and identifying characteristics of certain characters in order to protect the privacy of the potentially innocent.

# Contents

Notes from the Night

**1**

*The Day*

Those who dream of drinking wine may weep when morning comes.

—CHUANG TZU

HERE IN NEW YORK, a good night never ends. We will not let it. Though the hour is late, we are more awake than we have ever been in our lives, we are wild-eyed and grinning and dancing around like fools, and the music is thumping and the lights are flashing and the whole place is pulsating like a massive beating heart, and we do not want to go home, we do not want to go to sleep. Above all, we do not want to miss anything.

It hardly matters that the nightclub finally kicks us out. The lights back on, the music cut, its sudden absence ringing in our ears. The hulking bouncers herding us to the door: "You don't have to go home," they call out with those barrel-chested voices, "but you can't stay here." Even then, when we're pushed out into the strange predawn night—a twilight like dusk but darker, cleaner, bluer—even then, we will not let the night end. Indeed, it is at times like these, when anyone in their right mind would say, "It's four-thirty in the morning, I need to get the fuck to bed," that I sometimes hear my friend Zoo say, "Yeah, man, so what's next, man—I'm just getting started. . . ."

So we move things back to a late-night, to an after-party at my apartment, or someone else's, and there are cold cans of beer there, beautiful girls we hijacked from the last club, blaring music the neighbors must not even be able to comprehend—they must hear it and think it a dream—and though soon enough morning light comes streaming through the curtains, it is still the night because we have not slept.

Here in New York, a good night does not end until you sleep—if you sleep—and even then, in the morning, or the afternoon, when you awake, the taste of it is on your tongue and in your throbbing head. You stink of it—liquor and beer and cigarettes—and you carry that stench, and its accompanying hangover, with you into the following day. But a good night out stays with you in another way, too. Because the next day, there's this sense that you were on the verge of something, as if you almost got there, the night before, but didn't. As if you'd fought this epic battle, there in the deep New York night, but that nothing had been clearly won. And you think to yourself that if only the night had continued on just a couple more hours, there would have been something good that would have come of it, something certain and fulfilling and right, a victory of sorts. But the night ended too early, even though it ended too late, and so there remains this sense of something unfinished, of a search not quite complete. You know that there is more out there, you can feel it, all the endless possibilities of future nights, and you go to sleep satisfied that you will never be satisfied, you go to sleep—and then awake—with the wonderful, starving feeling that life is not over yet, and you are young.

And, of course, here in New York, a good night never ends because somehow another one is always just beginning.

## A NEW NIGHT DAWNS

Several hours later, my phone rings at work, and it is Zoo. You would think it would be a relief to hear from a good friend, but in this case, it's not. Part of the problem is that Zoo has a way of calling at the precise time when you least want to hear from him. Like when I am just drifting off into a lovely early-evening, post-work nap, or when I have sunk into my couch to watch a really funny episode of *The Simpsons,* or the first scene of a good movie. Or like now, when I am at the office, hung over as hell, and do not want to talk to anyone, least of all my cheery good friend:

"What's up what's up?" he says. "What's going on?"

I manage, somehow, to reply in the appropriate manner:

"Nothing, dude, what's going on with you?"

But I dread these calls, I really do. Because I know what the bastard is going to say next:

"Yeah, so what do you got lined up for this evening?"

And I want to say, *Dude, come on, we went out last night, it's one in the afternoon, my head is soaked thick with scotch and cigarettes, I feel like ass, how could I possibly already have plans for tonight, leave me the fuck alone, let me do my stupid work and drudge through this day so I can just go home and collapse on the couch in front of the TV and just fucking chill.* But instead I say:

"Not much, man."

"Yeah, I'm thinking about stepping out for a bit," he says. This, you will learn, is an understatement, and Zoo is full of them. Last night we stepped out for a bit, and were up past five in the morning. "What do you think? You up for it?"

And I pause for a second and shake my hurting head slowly and sigh, but there is a grin on my face beneath the pain, and even though I've been out two nights in a row and my body is drained almost to transparency and I know that going out again is the last thing in the world I need to do, I say, "I don't know, dude, maybe, dude, maybe— we'll see."

But this is not good enough for Zoo. "Come on, now, dude, it's *Thursday,*" he reminds me, and he says it with such conviction you almost consider it a valid point, but the fact of the matter is he would say the same thing if it was Tuesday: "Come on, now, dude, it's *Tuesday.*" The thing is, there is no way to argue with Zoo. His logic is circular, flawless, impenetrable. *Yes, Zoo, it is indeed Thursday, that I can't deny. But what about the fact that yesterday was Wednesday, and we were out all night, and what about Tuesday, my man, what about that,* I could say, but I don't. There is simply no way to win. Besides, I don't want to win. It is an obsession for me, this night. And it is not the alcohol that calls, or the drugs, or even the sex (far too infrequent). No, I am in love with possibility. *Tonight,* I cannot help but to think, *tonight could be the night.* Because heading out on the town, you never know what will happen, it could be anything, everything, and whatever it is, it is not this, this whining blue computer screen in front of me, the phones ringing, the halogen lights humming and buzzing and casting that dead light all around the office. Whatever Zoo has planned, it is not this, and though sometimes I feel like killing the bastard when he calls me, somehow all well-rested and chipper and buzzing with plans and possibilities, I know that he means well. And I know that whatever we end up doing, it'll be something.

## WORK—OR, ONE OF THE REASONS I ENJOY THE NIGHT BETTER THAN THE DAY

In these early-afternoon hours, when somehow my night has already reluctantly begun, the great nightclubs of New York are slumbering—big and empty and swept clean. In some of them, perhaps, a forbidden shaft of daylight squeezes through one of the frosted front windows, a slant in thick red curtains, and lands on the empty dance floor, sunlit fingers peeking in like dreams to the sleeping beasts. The day is night for these clubs, as it is for the people who frequent them, like me and Zoo.

Back in the day, Zoo could sleep like the dead—long, dreamless hours in which he'd grind his teeth with a dull, crunching, squeaking sound that sent pigeons outside his window fluttering toward the hills. Indeed, back then, when he was home for break from high school or college, it sometimes seemed that the only light Zoo ever saw was that of the dawn after a long night out, and it was this that would send him scurrying like a vampire for cover of shade-drawn darkness.

And me, well, I love the day and all, but I love the nights more, and it's possible, perhaps, that I have spent more of my life awake at night than during the day. (It is certain I have seen more dawns from staying up than from getting up.) At one in the afternoon, I prefer to be slumbering, or maybe awakening slowly to a coffee or a cold Coke and a smoke, lolling about in soft, lazy sunlight, awaiting the night.

Feeling as I do about this, it is perhaps not surprising that the majority of my days at the office are spent in misery, the seconds like drops of water hanging stubbornly to the lip of a faucet, refusing to fall. Those are the days when I'm not hung over. When I am hung over, strangely enough, the day moves faster. Sure, my brain may be swollen and pressing against the back of my eyes and my tongue may taste of liquor and ash and when I stand up from my desk the room may lurch and tilt, but at least it's a challenge—I can feel the strain and sweat of concentrating through this pain—at least I'm feeling something. Yes, for all its negative points, at least a hangover gives you something to do. And so I might even say that in some sort of masochistic way, I love the badass, haggard feeling of being hung over but doing your duty anyway. It is the nothing I hate. And the regular days at work, there is only this nothing, and I am just counting the seconds until the day is over and I can go home, and the night can begin.

Because on a good night out there is dancing and celebration, there is drink and laughter, there are good friends and unimaginable women—there are all the things you need to balance that dreary repetition of work and day. But the night is not just antidote, it is not only good because the days are bad. The night is night in and of itself, with or without the drudgery of day, and I can never get enough of it.

## THE ART OF RECOVERY

Of course, there are undoubtedly those days after when you have had quite enough of it. You would think that with all the goddamn time I've spent out at night, I would have figured out by now how to avoid a hangover, but I haven't, at least not completely. Sure, like everyone else, I have my methods—making sure to eat a good meal before I start drinking, balancing out each shot with a glass of ice water, chowing a five-in-the-morning bacon, egg, and cheese sandwich to soak up the rest of the booze, pounding a bottle of water before bed—but still sometimes the night is so long and filled with consumption that in spite of all one's countermeasures, a mean hangover is inevitable.

A true hangover can make you question your whole way of life. You look and feel like death, a pale wisp of a person, and quite frankly, death might be preferable. Every atom in your body feels poisoned. Your brain is swollen with alcohol and pressing against your skull, and when you move your head too quickly, the room spins in response. Waves of nausea ease up your spine, you get too hot and then too cold, you wrap yourself in a blanket and shiver and sweat. You are, quite simply, sick. These are the days you spend with your cheek cool against the ceramic toilet, the days when you are too hung over to even go back to sleep, which is the only thing in the world you really want to do.

Days like these, you're probably not on top of the world mentally, either. After all, if you feel like this now, chances are you were too drunk last night, swaying and spilling your drink and slurring scotch-scented words into the face of some pretty thing, and even if you can't remember exactly what you did, you're pretty damn sure you must have done something stupid—you're too hung over not to have. And so there is a sense of shame or guilt that can accompany this state, a recognition that in the black hole of last night something bad might have happened, and it is at times like these, with your face against the toilet and the great terror of the unremembered pounding through your head, that you might consider such extremes as never going out again, quitting drinking and drugging, getting your life together. Fortunately, by the time you feel truly better—some two days later—such thoughts, along with the pain that spurred them, have faded.

But those days of true incapacitation are the rare ones. Thanks to the preemptive strikes of ice water and food, most of my hangovers nowadays are manageable. After all, a well-timed hangover can be a joyful experience, if you know how to do it right. Waking up late in the Long Island summer after a rough Friday night, rolling leisurely out of bed into the soft, welcoming day. Slipping on shorts and flip-flops and grabbing grilled cheeses and fries and bubbling, cold Cokes at the local diner (and maybe even a side of bacon cheeseburger for good measure). Heading to the beach with your friends, where the water will be blue and cold and will wash half your hangover right away. Emerging from the sea happy as a wet dog to collapse on warm towels on the yellow sand amongst your good friends under the sun. And maybe in those precious moments when you are still cool from the sea and before it gets too hot, you'll slip off into a lovely little nap. Or maybe, breathing hard from the cold of the water, you'll dry your hands on your towel and roll up a doobie to pass around—Spanish-style, with a touch of tobacco—and there is nothing like a spliff to turn a nasty hangover into something soft and hazy, to turn nausea into grins. And then there is perhaps a Frisbee tossed around, or a football, and wagers made on beautiful women in bikinis ("I'll give you fifty bucks if you tackle that girl into the ocean"), and more swims and waves bodysurfed with the cool white rush of foam all around you. And then maybe later, when the heat fades, you'll go play some hoops at the little red schoolhouse in Sagaponack, sweat out the remainder of last night on the eight-foot basket that even you can dunk on—vicious two-on-two trash-talking games to eleven for the Championship of the World—and it's like being Shaq out there with that short hoop, and there are skyhooks and finger-rolls and alley-oops and slamdunks, and a sign on the schoolhouse that says, PLAYGROUND IS FOR CHILDREN 6–12. And after the game, to cool off, there will be one more swim at dusk, the sun setting and the water turning black, and then back home to flick on the tube, and nap out any remaining heaviness, until you are truly ready for the new night to begin. . . .

Of course, a more inactive recovery can be called for at times, too. A winter weekend in the city, sleeping late with the cold outside, emerging in the afternoon to find your buddy who crashed on the living-room couch sipping coffee and blearily watching some random bass-fishing show. Yes, a hangover is the perfect excuse to waste a wonderful day, to invite over the friends you went out with the night before and order in large greasy meals and watch five movies straight, to pass the pipe around and sink deeper and deeper into the couch until you hardly exist, happily stoned now and the hangover a warm blanket, a welcome reason to stay inside. Hangovers can be fun, after all, especially when shared with friends: a post-mission debriefing, like the day after you've gotten down from climbing a mountain, battered but contented to recall your misadventures on the peak. Bullshitting, groaning, sympathizing, bursts of laughter and reminiscence.

But even if the preemptive strikes of water and chow helped and your hangover isn't too bad, and even if you are with friends and laughing and giggling and carrying on, the day after can still be sad, somehow. In this state, hung over, your body exhausted, endorphins all used up, mind filled with the sweet memories of another night lost, you are fragile, eggshell-thin, and can easily crack. Even a cheesy commercial or the touching end to a bad comedy can bring strange tears to your eyes. Because there is an emptiness that can follow a big event—a sort of day-after blues. You are full of the most immediate kind of nostalgia—a longing for the night before. Because the party is over, and it will never happen again exactly the same. Because there were friends there you hardly see anymore, there were women there you could have loved, there was everything a good night can be . . . but none of it is left in the morning.

## THE STRANGEST OBLIGATION

Of course, I don't know what deep thing I'm expecting to find in the shallow New York night. It is without a doubt a strange place to look for answers. Indeed, one of the odd realities about this nocturnal world is that, with all it has to offer, you usually end up doing the same damn thing. The same damn places with the stunning women who won't give you a second glance (or maybe even a first), the repetitive songs thumping away, the same endless bullshit. The velvet ropes and the pissy foreign doormen with their haughty glances and the twelve-dollar watered-down cocktails and the assholes in tight, striped button-downs shoving you aside as they barrel their way across the dance floor, and the drugs and self-destruction and darkness.

In my long years of going out on the town, I have spent a small fortune—shouldn't I have something to show for it? All I have are memories, and even those are fuzzy. In the end, I have no proof that I am even looking in the right place. In fact, there is much evidence to support the contrary, that there is nothing of moral (or, for that matter, any kind of) value out in this club culture, that the night is all self and ego and money and drugs and violence and meaningless sex. Yes, the night can seem an unlikely place to look for things like love or enlightenment, an odd choice for church. But it is what I have chosen nonetheless.

And I am not alone.

What are we, fools? Well, maybe, yes, but it is not entirely our fault. After all, where else would we look? Are we to find love at laundromats and libraries? Is happiness hiding in power lunches and boardroom meetings? The night may be a horrible place to look for anything meaningful, but for many of us, it also seems the only place. Besides, people have been looking for answers in the wrong places forever—it might just be what humans do best. And so it is fitting, somehow, that we have continued this practice in the night. Here we are, as we have always been, stumbling around in the shadows, seeking something in the dark.

Please, don't get me wrong. There is no cultural revolution happening out in the night right now, none that I can see. We are not on the edge of anything bright. There is no Studio 54 with its free love and guiltless drugs and Warholian debauchery, there are no twenty-four-hour Party People or Sex Pistols, there is not even a Limelight anymore, with its transvestites in Santa Claus suits and innocent kids with pacifiers in their mouths dancing away in ecstasy. Besides, all of that ended as badly as it could, with AIDS and overdoses and corruption and murder, a string of proofs that nothing that begins in the night can ever really end well.

How will my night end? I cannot say. But it's already happening, I can feel it. I'm getting old—not *old,* shit, what am I, twenty-seven?—but old in the sense that the night is slipping away from me. I can't do it the way I used to, night after night after night, though I try my best. There's this kid in my office, an intern, and he's hip and tall and good-looking and wears an army jacket, and it seems almost every day he's handing coworkers pamphlets to this party or that, to concerts featuring angry young bands or all-night DJs from the UK, and every night he goes out all night, this kid, and yet somehow he's fresh as spring grass the next day, ready to do it again. Me, not so much. My body does not rebound so easily anymore. I am getting stiff, cranky, elderly. I do things like throw out my back while getting into a cab, or picking up my little half sisters to swing them around in the air. These are an old man's problems, and I am young. The night takes its toll. My throat is torn from all that smoke; my lungs are weary. I get strange kinks in my neck, mysterious bruises I cannot place. Sometimes, the day after a long night out, my kidneys ache.

My friends are getting old, too, though they might choose to call it "mature." Getting married, quitting drinking, quitting smoking, taking work seriously, getting their priorities straight, being responsible. All quite wise, sensible, grown-up things I want absolutely no part of. Yes, my friends are growing up, and I don't like it. Right now even Zoo has a girlfriend and a good, steady job. I do not know what the world is coming to.

And me, I'm still here, one of the last, hanging on to this life, reluctant to let go of all these good times, these happy youthful years.

But even me, well, despite all my complaints about my friends, I don't do my nights the way I used to, either. More often than not, the thought of another evening out makes my body cry *Nooooo!* as if it were about to witness its own assassination. Indeed, going out is usually the last thing I want to do, and so more and more these days I decline Zoo's invitations, I sit on my couch instead and stare at the TV and do nothing. And I love it. It is the perfect antidote to a night out on the town. It recovers you right. But it is pathetic, too, to have to nurse your wounds like that, and even more, the entropy of it, the wonderfully sickening movement toward nothing. No adventure in that, no possibility, no life: The night has ended before it began.

And so when my long day is done, I often feel the strange obligation to go out on the town, looking for something more. I see it as a responsibility of sorts, a thing I must do, even if I don't want to. Because even the possibility of losing it, of letting the night drift away like years do, and friends, and other things one has loved, it sickens me—to lose that last bastion of pleasure and hope and excitement, that last place where you can let loose and dance. But I haven't fucking lost it yet.

## ORIGIN THEORIES OF THE NIGHT

It's hard to say how I got here, to this point in my life, where what I do is go out at night, again and again, looking for something. Maybe it was passed down from my parents, who used to hit up Studio 54 in its heyday, and were known to throw some of Manhattan's most legendary parties. I still remember falling asleep as a little kid, the distant murmur of cocktail chatter rising and falling in my ears, as soothing as the sea.

There is certainly something to be said for the fact that my upbringing led me to this point—after all, this is what the young and privileged do in this town at night: They go out. Yes, I could say that it was born in me, that I have always loved the night, but that would be untrue. It scared me at first, as it does perhaps all children—the cracked doors of closets and the spaces beneath beds, impossible things all too possible in the dark. I remember thinking that if something happened, some unspeakable dark thing, that I would want someone there, my mom or dad, to bear it with me, so I wouldn't have to face it alone. The night can be frightening when you're on your own, no doubt. It hardly matters whether you're six or twenty-six. Just a couple years back I spent a week by myself in the Ventana Wilderness, near Big Sur, California, and it scared the shit out of me. Sitting alone in the big forest night with my little campfire before me, I wasn't concerned by the thought of some mountain lion or *Deliverance*-style rapist wandering the woods looking for a victim (though that would have made a lot more sense), but rather by the simple fact that in the moonless, forested night, the pines looming up above me, I could not see a thing. Beyond the little illumined circle of my campfire, there was only the black night and the unnameable sounds coming out of it. And such darkness breeds imagination; every snap of a twig or rustle of leaves became something unspeakable—gremlins sharpening their claws against the bark of trees, the heavy breathing of something large and hairy, all of it way too possible when you're alone and there's no one there to reassure you. Even here and now, with my roommate, Hobbes, in the next room and this city of millions slumbering happily all around me, I still find myself afraid at times, lying in bed with the covers pulled up to my chin and eyes wide open, hearing things that don't sound right—the turning of a door handle, the creaking of a floorboard under something heavy—and with big eyes staring blindly into the darkness, I will take the tai chi saber down from my wall and creep out into the dark hall, my heart beating a mile a minute, only to discover Hobbes in his pajamas, calmly pouring himself a glass of milk.

Yes, it is no wonder that when the light of day fails, we gather together to ward off the darkness with laughter and good cheer. It is a herd mentality, a kind of rollicking safety in numbers, a biological imperative that must stretch back to the caveman days:

"Hey, Thag, it's kinda dark and scary. Wanna hang out, build a fire, dance around it or something?"

"Sounds good to me."

So it is that I must trace my love for the night to when I no longer had to face it alone, to when I was old enough to have sleepovers with friends. It was then, with the courage that comes with companionship, that I began to explore the evening's edges. Staying up way past bedtime plotting math-class spitball attacks and whispering devious plans for summer break, going on missions through dark living rooms to kitchens where forbidden cookies lay, waging massive battle-royale pillow fights that ended in bloody noses and aching heads, heaving water balloons and soggies out windows at cars and helpless pedestrians on the streets far below. And on Long Island in the summer, we'd leave body-shaped lumps of pillows under the covers of our beds and sneak out through wooden doors that always creaked too loud onto night-blue roads, hiding in bushes when cars gloomed by, and we'd steal road signs to hang on our bedroom doors that said DO NOT ENTER and DEAD END, just like in the movies.

And later, there were seventh- and eighth-grade dances, where all the boys and girls from the city schools would get together and stand around awkwardly, and there were crushes, and French kisses, and this sudden longing I had never known. These were the years we began to smoke cigarettes, and we would sneak out into the illicit New York night, not to do anything really, just to be out there, sitting on stoops smoking butts and feeling cool, prowling about looking for trouble, still a bit too young to hit up the bars, but we could see them, sense them—the beautiful women stumbling out from music-filled places, their laughter and liquor-rosed cheeks drifting down the streets. Even then we could sense our future.

And then in boarding school, back in the city for vacations, there were parties and people were drinking vodka and smoking pot, and in a world where everything was school and structure and parents and rules, the night was suddenly open and ours, if still illicit. So we'd go to Chinese restaurants where we'd be served without being carded, slurp up big, fruity alcoholic drinks out of crystal bowls with straws, and there were bars that didn't card, too, cool little places on the Upper East Side where all the high-school kids went, and there were women all of a sudden (or something like them), all these girls with their swelling breasts and fresh young faces, and people would make out in the corners, girls' tongues tasting of vodka and cinnamon gum.

These were the years we would stumble along streets, puke in bathrooms, regurgitate shots of Cuervo right back out onto bars, testing our limits and failing, again and again and again. And it always seemed like someone had a house where there were no parents, or the parents didn't care, and so there were parties, good ones, the first real parties of our lives, and there was sex, too, awkward and thrilling and dangerous, and everything was fresh and new and not a one of us knew what the hell we were doing, but we all pretended we did, and we pushed it as far as we could. Sitting on the center median of Park Avenue doing bong hits, hitting up the Limelight on Ecstasy, staying up till dawn on my rooftop tripping on LSD, the morning light easing through the never-quite-dark New York night, and it was all not allowed, none of it, we were breaking the rules, all of them, and we loved it.

And that still holds true today—you go out for a night on the town and you know you shouldn't, and that's part of why you go: Still there is that illicit thrill of disobeying the cycles of Mother Nature and common sense, of heading out into the dark and dangerous night just because it's there.

## AMBASSADOR ZOO

Before the day is done, I expect at least three more calls from Zoo to keep me updated on any developments with his grandiose plans. His calls always come at a bad time, and worse, his updates are usually devoid of any real information, and his questions are mostly rhetorical.

"So what do you think, dude?" *Chomp, chomp, chomp.* Zoo is always snacking on something when he calls. You can hear him munching away, pausing between bites to toss out a useless comment or question. "I don't know, so, yeah, dude"—*chomp, chomp*—"what do you think?"

"I don't know, man. . . . What are you chowing?"

*Chomp, chomp*—"Sandwich." *Crunch, crunch*—"Chips."

Linguine with white clam sauce, Philly-cheese-steak grinders, chicken salad sandwiches—Zoo will eat anything he can get his hands on. He's only really happy if he has at least five or six feasts a day. It's not uncommon to hear him say, as he's smacking his lips on something, "Yeah, dude, I've only had three meals today. I could use a steak."

If Zoo were an animal, he'd be a panther, all sleek and long and dark. Lounging about in trees napping all day in the dappled canopy light. Awaking groggily at dusk, stretching, yawning a big cat yawn, descending lazily to prowl the jungle night looking for good times and snacks.

Zoo's parents are foreign-born, but he is first and foremost a New Yorker. He is a master of wearing black, as all true New Yorkers are—the black shoes and the ubiquitous black blazer that he wears over a crisp button-down. He is tall and lean and handsome, and his hair is short with just a hint of hip spike to it, though he often crushes it down with a black baseball cap. We've been best friends since high school, and throughout this time he has been my connection to a side of this city I never really knew before I met him. Long ago he introduced me to the word "Word?" and to "I'm down with that" and "Peace" before I'd heard them anywhere else, even in the movies. One of his latest is "Yao Ming," a condensed version of "Do you know what I mean?" as in, "The shit's gonna be hot tonight, yao ming yao ming?" Oddly, for one so well-versed in the slang of the streets, he also says the word *dude* more than anyone else I know, although he has a way of saying it that is purely New York, with a certain harshness, as if it is more an admonishment than a stoned, fuzzy calling, as in "Dude, fuck that, man, whatever, dude."

But above all, Zoo has been my link to the club scene, my ambassador to the night. Any new place that opens up, he's on it. He knows the names of all the owners and promoters and bouncers at all the hottest spots, the places where celebrities can be found dancing on plush red couches in the VIP room, or where Mark Ronson or Q-Tip might take a spin on the turntables for the pleasure of the crowd, or where stunning little actresses can be seen laughing their little-girl laughs, and breaking the hearts of men like me who can only watch from the balcony with a longing that is far greater than our distance—and there is nothing Zoo enjoys more than showing up at a club like this where the line outside is twenty, fifty deep and the velvet ropes are as formidable as concrete, strolling casually past the restless, angry crowd, right up to the front, where he'll give one of the doormen a nod and a pat on the back and a big old friendly grin and say, "What's going on, man, things good? Yeah, it's just the two of us," and the velvet ropes part like some slender red sea.

Yes, I cannot imagine a better guide to nightlife than Zoo, and yet you must not allow this statement to give you the wrong idea. There is nothing underhanded about the Zoo. That Hollywood image of the pale, vampiric night crawler, oozing his way into VIP rooms and women's panties, the eight ball of coke in his jacket pocket—that is not Zoo. No, Zoo is just Zoo, a genuine article, an original. And strangely enough, the reason he's so adept at the night is exactly this—he's genuine. There's nothing false in his smiles or in his rap, he's just being himself; it just so happens that he's got such a positive, easygoing way of carrying himself that his presence is disarming, even to huge bouncers stacked to the teeth with muscles and cynicism. Yes, it is near impossible not to like Zoo. He's a good kid, and he's a good friend.

Of course, like any good friend, Zoo can be confounding. You know him too well for him not to be. You know the contradictions. Like the fact that he smokes at least a pack of Camel Lights a day (and bums his fair share of American Spirits from you) but somehow also manages to do some crazy Navy SEAL boxing workout. Or the fact that he can drink like a fish, but that seeing him drunk is a rare thing indeed. (The times he does get sloshed, he is a happy, rowdy drunk, all smiles and laughter and trouble.) Yes, you know that Zoo can be quite shy around women, though at the same time he loves nothing more than to be surrounded by them. You know that he is all New York but somehow ended up going to college in New England, where he was forced to rule the tame rural nightlife like a king in exile. You know that he knows his hip-hop cold but has a soft spot for heavy metal, Brazilian jazz, the Grateful Dead. You know he likes to plan things early but will undoubtedly always be late. And you know that one of his favorite phrases is, "Dude, trust me," said with such emphatic self-confidence that you want to believe him, even though you know you shouldn't—not because he is lying to you, but just because sometimes Zoo is wrong, even if he's positive he's not. And knowing all this, you know that you can never be sure of anything with Zoo. Yes, like the night, Zoo is a mystery, a conundrum, and just the thought of him is enough to get me and my other friends smiling and shaking our heads in familiar disbelief.

## THE ART OF PREPARATION

As soon as I can, I break out from work. There are things to be done before the night truly begins. Like napping. So that is what I do when I get home, I toss on *The Simpsons* and sprawl out on my couch and nap to episodes I have seen before. Disco naps, I've heard them called. And yes, I do love the sinking darkness and finger-twitching half-dreams of a well-deserved snooze, but the main reason I nap at this hour is that there is a long night ahead, and I need my energy. It is always in one's best interest to be well rested for an evening out with the Zoo.

I am usually just drifting off when he calls again, just to see what's going on. "What's up? How are ya? How are things? What's goin' on?"

"Nothing, dude, just taking a nap." He must hear the exasperation and exhaustion in my voice, and this would make most people say, "Sorry, dude, why don't you give me a call back when you wake up," but Zoo is not a normal person, and it doesn't seem to faze him. So instead he says, "Yeah, so, dude, we got shit going on tonight." And then there is the list, the names and places, the endless options. About which, frankly, I couldn't care less.

Generally, these days, I try to stay out of the planning process, and do my best to keep things simple. It is not wise, for instance, to try to organize your average night with too many people. Zoo isn't the only person I have heard from throughout the day. Fatdog is meeting two chicks for drinks in Alphabet City, wants me to join him—"They're cute, Tap, you should really come down and meet us," he says. My roommate, Hobbes, is going out for ribs and beer with Whitey, invited me along. Stibbs is going to dinner with his woman, might want to meet up with us later. Tako, the madman, is back in town from L.A. And my oldest friend, G, a big bear of a guy, is in from the 'burbs for dinner with this crazy comedian Benny, and they could be down for something, too. And I could try to organize it all and make it happen—and sometimes we do go out as a big rollicking group—but it is easier to simply head out with the Zoo, let the rest fall into place as it will. Besides, Zoo's already talked to everyone, somehow has everything figured out. "Don't worry about it, dude," he says. "We'll meet up with those herbs later when they're done doing their nonsense."

It is always easiest to travel the night in twos. With two, it is just you and your wingman. You are mobile, open to the night and the directions it leads you. Things are simple. You are on a mission, the two of you—to have a good time—and there is little that can stop you. But try organizing a night out with a full-on posse, and things get complicated. After all, one of the reasons the night is supposedly such a great antidote to a long day at work is that this is your time, and you are free to do as you wish. But when too many people get involved, you can easily end up wasting your whole evening zigzagging manically from spot to spot, rushing to get to all the places you said you'd go and meet all the people you said you'd see, overcommitted and underpleased.

You can wreck a night with expectations and organizations. Indeed, it is the big nights out, the ones you'd think would be the best, the New Year's Eves and Fourth of Julys, that always end up sucking, somehow. The night, I have learned, has its own plans. If you hope for too much from it or attempt to wrestle it into the shape you think it should take, you will undoubtedly find yourself disappointed. And so most of the time I just plan to meet up with Zoo, leave the rest to fate.

But the truth of the matter is that I avoid the organization process not only out of wisdom, but because being an organizer just isn't part of my personality: I have enough trouble simply coordinating myself. I spend a ridiculous amount of time getting ready, showering, shaving, trying on one thing and then the other. Four different button-downs, two pairs of pants, black shoes, brown shoes. Attempting rather feebly to figure out which sock is for which foot. (I once told a rather stylish girl how much effort I put into my outfits. She looked me up and down—I think I was wearing khakis and sneaks and an old camel-hair coat—and advised me never to tell anyone this ever again.)

Unlike Zoo, I am far from New York cool. I have no sense of style, really, beyond the cold facts of matching shoes and belt, and I usually turn to Hobbes—who always seems to be sporting the Diesel jeans and old-school Adidas or Puma sneaks—for final confirmation on whether or not my costume for the night cuts it. (Never mind the fact that most of these places are so dark no one can see what you're wearing anyway, nor the fact that whatever nice thing you're wearing that no one can see is bound to get splattered by the muck of the night: This is New York, and we want to look good.) Often, these days, I'll end up wearing a dark suit with some sort of funky-collared button-down beneath. Maybe a tie, loosely knotted, for fun. Part of the reason is that it is easy to wear a suit (you can't go wrong, as they say), but mostly it's because I work at a place where the norm is jeans and a T-shirt, and I enjoy dressing up. It makes you feel like you're going somewhere, even if you're not. Besides, my scruffy appearance—often unshaved, a mess of too-long, curly blond hair, a goofy grin—is balanced nicely by a fine suit.

Yes, as much as Zoo is New York, I am something else. I am no player, no master of the night. It is more fate than personality that led me to my position as a frequenter of the whole club scene. I am no good at talking the talk, whether it be to a six-foot bouncer or a six-foot blonde. I do not own a black T-shirt or a gold chain, and my cell phone goes unused for days on end. Until a couple years ago, I didn't even own a pair of black boots.

Strangest of all, I've spent a lot of my life craving solitude, and fulfilling that craving: wandering off into this forest or that with just the pack on my back, imagining that out there in the wilderness, alone, I might finally find myself, the me that had nothing to do with the social world, the me that was simply me. Which, of course, was mostly a whole lot of nonsense. You are, after all, always who you are, no matter where you are, and attempting to find one's self is like looking for a pair of glasses you're already wearing. But though I found very little out there in the wilds, nonetheless I loved the adventure in it, the search. I loved the feeling of heading out there into the unknown.

For me, the city night is not so different. Though this immensely social world may be an unlikely place for a solitude-seeking cat like me—some of the clubs I've been to pack in more than two thousand people—there's a sense in which the night is simply another wilderness: I am heading off on an adventure, and anything could happen. And so getting ready for an evening out on the town, it's as if I am packing for a journey to the ends of the earth. I am struck with a nervous flutter of anticipation, with a grand sense of something about to begin, I am showering and shaving and smacking aftershave on my face, the phone is ringing and the beats are bumping and I am dancing around in my towel and generally making a fool of myself, doing the mambo in front of mirrors, I am flinging clothes around and trying on one outfit and then the next and digging through unmatchable socks, I am smoking cigarettes and sipping a bourbon on the rocks and feeling the warmth in my stomach spread, and my windows over Sixth Avenue are thrown open to the big city night awaking from its slumber, the cabs tooting and the squeal of brakes and the laughter of girls moving down the streets in groups, and SUVs with bright rims rolling by bumping a bass so loud I can feel it in my organs, and everyone is going somewhere, and I am about to go somewhere, too—my night is about to begin.

## ZOO AND THE ART OF PATIENCE

When I'm finally ready to go, I give Zoo a call. We were originally planning on meeting up around 10:30, but it's already 10:10 and he is eating some sort of a sandwich or leftover Chinese food—his fourth meal of the day, at least—and is nowhere close to ready. "Yeah, dude, just have to finish chowing and hop in the shower. I'll be ready in twenty."

There is a formula you can apply to Zoo's estimates of when he'll be ready. Take the number he tossed out there, multiply it by five, subtract the original number from it, and divide by the square root of negative fifteen. In other words, you never know when the guy will show up. His sense of punctuality is so chronically screwed up that he even arrives early every now and then, a final sign that there is no real method to his madness, only chaos. Of course, I understand how it happens. (I'm always late, too.) He doesn't mean to be tardy, he just makes bad estimates of how long it takes him to do stuff. You know, he finishes his sandwich, lingers on the chips. This itself takes twenty minutes: Zoo chews his food. Afterward, he will light up a smoke and kick back. (This will take at least another ten minutes: I don't know anyone who smokes lengthier cigarettes than Zoo.) And then after his smoke he probably picks his clothes, and hops in the shower and shaves and hooks up his hair and all that, which is at least another half hour, and so before he's even ready to leave the house, he's already forty minutes late. Of course, he didn't mean to be, and so if you give him shit when he finally arrives, strolling in without an ounce of guilt on his face, as if he hadn't just devoured some canary (which in his mind, he hasn't), his response will most likely be, "Dude, whatever, dude," to which there is no appropriate reply. Besides, he's done this to you for so many years now that you can't help but forgive him even as you curse him. After all, you knew damn well when he said twenty he meant an hour, even if he didn't. In fact, all things considered, he's probably early.

The thing is, much of the night besides Zoo is also about waiting. Waiting for the sun to sink, the day to end, the night to begin. Waiting in lines to get in, or get out, or for the bathroom, or for your drinks. Waiting for that one song, that one woman, that one moment. Indeed, there is so much waiting in the night that putting up with Zoo is good practice, a kind of Buddhist penitence, a maddening koan, its purpose to instill ultimate resignation. . . .

But then there are moments of true movement, of action. Like when we finally meet up and get a few quick drinks in us at some pre-game spot and hop in a cab and give the guy the address. And if we are uptown and going down, Zoo will say, "Sir, take the FDR Drive," and then say, "Sir, does your radio work?" (he will ask this even if the radio is already working, because in Zoo's mind if it's not tuned to something he wants to be hearing, it's not actually functioning correctly) and then say, "92.3" or "104.3" or "97.1," or maybe he'll have his iPod and iTrip with him tucked away in his blazer pocket, and the beats will come on, and Zoo will say, "Turn it up." And we'll hit the Drive, the East River speeding by on our left, or perhaps we'll take an avenue instead and catch the crest of lights turning green, and Zoo will say, "Sir, do you mind if we smoke— big tip, big tip," and we will unroll the windows and light up our smokes, and the driver will be zooming past the other cars, no one like the yellow cab drivers of New York, driving in bursts that throw you back against the cushioned seat, and we are nodding our heads to the rhythm of the beats and the guy's driving, and the wind is in our hair and the green lights are spreading out before us, and we are going somewhere, downtown into the heart of the New York night, lower Manhattan, and even if you are going to the same old place, it feels like you are going somewhere you've never been.

**2**

*Place and Time—or, Why Einstein
Might Have Stayed Home*

Meet me at no special place, and I'll be there at no particular time.

—NAT KING COLE

**HERE IN NEW YORK,** you could literally go to a place you have never been every single night for the rest of your life. This is not only because there are well over a thousand places to go, but because these spots are constantly closing and new ones are opening in their stead, so that the options in New York are practically infinite.

Chamber music, death metal; jazz club, S&M club. You could hit up a rock concert in a grand old ballroom where seven thousand too-cool kids in trucker's caps and superfluous secondhand clothes will be nodding their heads in unison to the beat, or you could seek out one of those fat Cuban joints where people really dance, well-groomed Latino men and luscious Latina girls shaking it as only they know how, twirling and stepping and clapping their hands, little skirts flying. You could do the rave thing, the DJs from the UK and Holland spinning edgy techno beats in cavernous clubs, thousands of kids with lollipops and pacifiers in their mouths and in their eyes ecstasy and lights flashing; or you could park yourself with a couple buddies in an old-school Irish pub with sawdust and peanut shells on the floor and a gruff waiter who will respond to your request for a glass of water by looking at you like you've got a screw loose and saying, "One light beer, coming up." You could consider a karaoke bar, a strip club, the Blue Man Group. There are classy midtown champagne lounges bathed in red candlelight that play Dave Matthews, and where couples have close conversations over tall, thin glasses, there are badass biker bars over by the Hudson, all leather and beer and whiskey and big bearded faces in the night. On Wednesdays there is roller disco at the Roxy, Texas Hold 'Em tournaments at underground poker clubs. There are the Upper East Side bars packed with high-school and college kids home from break, all happy hours and baseball caps, there are goth clubs where men in leather hoods kneel in corners, fat women in spandex short-shorts striking them with whips as vampire techno thumps away like the beating of a rabid heart.

And what an adventure it would be to attempt this, to do something different, something new, every night. I wish I could tell you that my nightlife was as rich as the city's: that on Tuesdays I see the symphony, and on Wednesdays I suck the toes of a busty dominatrix; that on Thursdays I do Ecstasy and dance till dawn in mysterious Jersey warehouses, and on Fridays recover by falling in love with some sweet thing at a bowling alley downtown. I wish I could tell you that I take advantage of all this city has to offer and saw more concerts, more guerilla theater, more poetry jams, but I do not.

Now, this is partly just a natural human response to the sublime—there's so much out there, you kind of have to disregard the majority of it, if only for your own sanity—but it is also the curse of the homegrown New Yorker, or of any native of a tourist destination. Much the way some Caribbean islanders condescend to the sea, never bothering to learn how to swim, so it is with us—we tend to shun our city's grand attractions, its wealth of culture, its famous monuments and skyscrapers. Instead, we find places we can call our own.

Yes, everyone's got their individual spots in New York. Especially a cat like Zoo. He has his rounds, the places he will or will not go, and it's not really up for discussion.

"Hey, Zoo, want to go to a goth bar?"

"Yeah, right. That's pretty funny, you monkey."

See, the thing is, Zoo is a firm believer in the theory that of all these possibilities, all the endless options this thick night offers, there is nonetheless a right place to go, a "place to be"—and so, for the most part, it is only to these hotspots, all abuzz and sizzling like live wires, that we are drawn.

Which is why I often wonder what the hell we're doing here. Yes, considering the fact that Zoo is all about the place to be, it consistently amuses (and annoys) me that before we head downtown into the heart of the city darkness, he makes me meet him at Lux, an upper-midtown lounge that, though it's certainly classy enough (and, in this top-shelf sort of way, fits Zoo perfectly), could never be considered hip. Oh, it's a nice place and all—they have a big guy at the entrance armed with red ropes, and every now and then someone will have a party there and it will be a rocking time—but mostly it is very tame. Nowadays the place pulls in more of an after-work crowd than anything else, the midtown business folk needing an early-evening drink to help shrug off office memories, and by the time Zoo and I meet up there—it's probably 11:15—the place is half empty, the beautiful waitresses in their black dresses hanging out and talking to bartenders, maybe twenty or so people lining the bar and lounging at tables, maybe one or two pretty civilians, nothing very much worth it at all. I often attempt to argue this case to Zoo, that it makes no sense for me to come all the way up here when I live downtown and forty minutes later we'll be heading right back down there to somewhere much cooler, but any argument is of course useless—Lux is just his hangout, it's where he starts his nights, and that's the way it is. "I'll cover your drinks for you, dude," he says, as if that will convince me. It usually does.

Not that it's any real skin off his back. After all, Zoo's been frequenting this spot for so long now, two or three nights a week since it opened, that he's basically best buddies with the whole management, all the doormen and bartenders and waitresses, all the bouncers and busboys and managers. Shit, he even went to grade school with the owners. And as with any place where everyone knows your name, there are benefits, free drinks, discounts; Zoo is treated well and he treats them well in return, gives them big tips, big, friendly grins and handshakes, his big, friendly presence. Yes, Zoo isn't a bad regular to have at a joint. Hip and tall and handsome, he makes a place look good just by being there, and of course he brings them more tangible benefits as well: mainly, me and all his other friends who don't get drinks for free.

So considering how well Zoo is treated at Lux, it's not a

bad spot to get things going. Even if it is a little empty by the time we get there, it's not a bad place to have on lockdown: large and dim and comfortable, the beautiful waitresses sashaying about, the DJ not bad, the drinks cheap and strong, the bartenders friendly and knowing what you want before you've even told them. And I guess that's what it's become for us, a local dive bar of sorts (yes, and it forever amuses me that this place, Lux, with its velvet ropes and doormen, is as close to a dive as Zoo ever gets—as if the very fact that they do have velvet ropes is enough for him to overlook the plain truth that most of the time, the ropes are guarding nothing of real value).

## THE PLACE TO BE?

It's hard to say what the place to be actually is, or if it even really exists. One thing is for certain: Lux is not it.

As far as I can tell, the place to be is not actually one place, though it might as well be. No, there are probably up to ten hotspots we frequent at any one time—and there have perhaps been hundreds over the years—but the differences between them seem minimal. They all have the same velvet ropes, the same discerning doormen, the same beautiful women. Yes, this is the place where the line to get in will be deep and going nowhere, this is the place where the doormen will probably be foreign and pissy and dressed impeccably in dark suits and fatly knotted ties, this is the place where the women inside (if you can get inside) will be so beautiful that the sight of them will make you want to howl like a forlorn coyote, hurl prayers and curses at a god whose existence you must question for having put these untouchable creatures before you.

These spots even have names that sound alike: the shorter the better, punchy and with a little zip, as if your average night owl could only be expected to remember monosyllables (though of course this has had the opposite effect, making the mass of monosyllabic names—Flow, Show, Blo, etc.—nearly impossible to distinguish). The names also tend to offer something spiritual at times, as if upon entering, some ancient, hidden mystery will be revealed—Ohm, Lotus, Pangaea, Tao—simple words that evoke grand concepts: the primordial sound of the universe, the Buddhist symbol for enlightenment, the great landmass of earth before it broke up into the continents, the unseen, unnameable force out of which all is born. Yes, incongruous as it may seem, these places speak of religion, as if they are not so much nightclubs as they are dark churches, looming in the night, packed with wild-eyed fanatics dancing to some ancient horned god.

Other names can be counted on to offer you something hidden in a different way: They evoke something regal and exclusive—Marquee, Bungalow 8, Suite 16, Lot 61—almost as if, through their very specificity, they leave little doubt that they are the place to be, like you had been slipped the hotel room number where the sick after-party will be, or given the address, in hushed tones, of the deserted warehouse where the most outlandish bash of the year will be held. As if you and only you had been let in on some great secret.

This is what these places promise that nowhere else in New York can: a feeling of exclusivity. The easiest way to describe the clubs we go to is that they are selective—not everyone who tries to will get in. And though this is of course part of what makes these places irresistible, I don't entirely buy it. I mean, just because their gates are guarded, does that mean that what lies behind them is necessarily worthwhile?

No—I cannot tell you with any certainty that I have chosen the right kind of place. You can, after all, have yourself a great night no matter where you go: dive bar, strip club, ratty basement lounge; conversely, hit up the hottest party of the evening, and you may find yourself in an hour-long line to get in, if you can get in, and if and when you do, no way to move in there, everything too hot and everyone too close and shoving and trying to get places and going nowhere, frustration on their faces, the bathroom line fifteen minutes long, to get a simple drink at the bar, even longer. Why bother?

I have many friends who scoff at the hassled hotspots I go to, all their velvet-rope VIP nonsense, and I don't blame them. Take my oldest buddy in the world, for instance, G. He is most at home barreling through snow-struck woods on skis, or casting for stripers in wild Atlantic surf—and when I spoke to him earlier tonight, mentioned that Zoo had plans to do the whole club thing, he emitted a low, guttural growl . . . "Yeah, we *could* do that," he said, "or we could do something that's *actually* fun—like grab some beers and just fucking *chill*." Yes, G prefers your average dive bar, a place where the music isn't so loud and you can actually have a conversation. And G is not alone. Everyone complains about the whole nightclub scene. It is indeed an easy target: the pissy door policies, the ridiculously priced cocktails, the ample posturing of its crowd, the music overplayed, the women so practiced in boredom and beauty they almost might as well not exist.

The places I go, as much as they are marked apart by

their exclusivity, are also marked by it. I mean, shouldn't we be evolved enough by now to have said good-bye to such elitism? These moonlit paradises, these false little heavens of the night, everything set exactly in such a way that there is nothing to make one feel uncomfortable, everything and everyone beautiful—shit, even the bar backs are handsome. Yes, this is the elite, the few, the oligarchy of the night, and it's a bit disgusting. Oh, it's beautiful, but the things it requires to make it so, its methods, are ugly. Like some fucking country club for the young. Except it's not based so much on race—I have never seen anyone denied at the door because of creed or color—as it is on some strange status of the night, some elusive dark cool.

The result is that there can be something too finished about these clubs. Or rather, there is something more innocent about the unexclusive places, where it is not so much about getting in as it is about actually being there, having a good time. Five bucks at the door and an ID and anyone can come inside. Because there it's not about who's who or if you're important enough to even get in, it's just good people out for good fun. And the outcome is something truer, something closer to what the night is really about: everyone dancing and drinking and carrying on like they don't have a care in the world. But at the clubs I frequent, there can be a kind of socially imposed self-consciousness, an awareness of eyes on you, of how you must look, your movements therefore guarded, your spirit somehow caged.

Yes, I admit it: There is something wrong with the places I go, and it's not easy to put a finger on. I was talking to one girl who said she couldn't stand these venues but wasn't able to explain exactly why. All she knew was that as soon as she walked into a hotspot, she immediately wanted to leave. It wasn't even the people—she said if it had been the same crowd somewhere else, at a house party, for instance, the scene would have been fine. No, it was as if the place itself was evil, a haunted palace that fed on bringing out the worst in people. This is what she said, finally, the closest she could come to the truth: *People are at their worst in a place like that.* Everyone looking for something better to do, somewhere better to be, someone more important to talk to, everyone putting on airs and puffing themselves up and looking down on it all with narrow, shifty eyes. As if from the moment we arrive at its guarded gates, we are infused with something foul, transformed into creatures we never really wanted to be.

Of course, realizing all this hasn't stopped me. Somehow, I manage to maintain a kind of stubborn hope for these places I go. I have to believe, if only for my own sanity, that there's something else out there in all that glamour and glitz and possibility, some chance for something bigger than you can get anywhere else, some kind of perfect American dream. . . . Yes, I have to believe in this life, these people: After all, this is my life, and these people are me.

But I do wish there were a happy medium of sorts. I am a romantic. I want everything. I want a place G and Zoo would enjoy equally, a place that does not, as far as I know, exist. Perhaps it never could. Yes, if I had a club, it would probably never work. My club would have no door policy, no metal detectors or ropes, the bouncers would blend into the shadows. Everyone would be on equal footing; anyone could come and anyone could go. There would be a big room with a DJ and a dance floor, a raised level or two, a balcony for looking down, deep, comfortable couches. The music would always be good, and beautiful women would always be dancing, which means so would everyone else. There would be no VIP room. Instead, there would be a courtyard, or a roof deck, with trees and sky, couches and tables, another bar, another DJ, room for a band. On Tuesdays there would be live salsa up there, on Thursdays there would be reggae. There would be a grill under the stars for late-night cheeseburgers. The drinks would be cheap and strong. There would be a lethal house rum punch, its exact ingredients known only by me. Pretty bartenders would serve it up with a smile and a warning. The lighting would be dim and red, giant plants would sprout out of corners, the walls would be layered, sliding, so that you could go from Miami white to deep midnight blue, depending on the night. Zoo would be my consultant, and would tell me how little of this could ever work. How I would need a guy at the door to keep out the riffraff, promoters to invite the cool crowd in . . . lists, VIP rooms, investors, bottle service. I would respond, hopefully, that if the place was right, all of that stuff would be irrelevant. Yes, it wouldn't matter who came in—disarmed by the casualness of the place, they would have no choice but to simply kick back and enjoy themselves. People would feel more than welcome, as if they had finally gotten home after a long day of work. There would be artists there, and writers, and musicians, there would be Wall Street fools and cats from the Bronx, there would be cute girls in from Japan and Jerusalem and Jersey, there would be everyone there, each not at all like the other and yet right here, right now, all together in this one funky place, all just out to have a good time. My club would be a safety zone, a place where people could finally be themselves. And I would wander the premises, invisible, pausing to shake it a bit on the dance floor when an exceptionally fat beat filled the room, shooting chilled shots at some table in the corner with Zoo and the boys, greeting my guests when it seemed appropriate. . . . I imagine myself a proud father of sorts, happy to have created a place that made people happy, content to see his children dance.

I have to believe that the extended crowd I roll with in New York would be cool enough to realize that my place, though it wouldn't actually be exclusive, would still be cool, cooler even, but I don't know if they would. I see Zoo dropping by for an early-evening cocktail and then making excuses to slip off to someplace else. . . .

If I had a place, it would probably never last.

## TIME, AND THE ELUSIVE PARTY

I could tell you which places are the hotspots right now, but there would be little point. By the time you read this, the list would be outdated. (Shit, by the time *I* know about it, it's almost outdated.) Time ruins all in New York. Nothing lasts.

Take this place Float, for instance, where we used to chill on Thursday nights. And this was a *club*, with a big dance floor and bumping beats and beautiful half-naked go-go dancers writhing in cages floating in the corners above the dance floor and lights and lasers flashing, and an upstairs area where you could overlook the frenetic ground floor and get a closer look at the dancers in their cages, and this was one VIP room, the upstairs balcony, but then behind closed doors up there, there was a second VIP room, and upstairs from there, a third, and beyond that, up a final narrow wooden staircase, even a fourth, so that in this one club there was always someplace cooler you could go, four levels of hipness, and we'd hit this place up and Zoo and I would lean over the balcony nodding our heads to the scene below and groove to the beats and ascend the VIP rooms, and this was the kind of place you could see yourself going infinitely, because it seemed it always had something new, something even more secret, to offer. . . .

But then, as time passed, you could see the place get a little more cheesy, more guys in tight T-shirts and chains and women with big hair and boobs, and other nights it would be suddenly thin, this grand place, lights and lasers flashing on an empty dance floor. And then we just stopped going, no real conscious decision, just the way it happened, as if the path we followed had swerved in another direction, and now I have not been there in years, though it's still there, and someone, I imagine, must still be going, just not me. For me, Float has sunk. It's another club now, has got another name. For all I know, it's cool again.

What makes a place fade from the limelight is not an easy thing to latch on to. It is random, given, inevitable. This is simply what happens to places: They get tired, old, finished, done. They have their moment, if they're lucky enough to have their moment, and then that moment passes. Imagine a time lapse of bars and clubs opening and closing in New York and it would be like fireflies in the night.

Of course, sometimes it's obvious why a place shuts down—the greed of Steve Rubell at Studio 54, or the excessive drugs and violence associated with the Limelight—but most disappear more quietly. And sure, there are reasons to point to, why these places die and how: They weren't exclusive enough, they were too exclusive, it was the wrong business plan, the wrong location, the wrong layout, the wrong music, the wrong crowd. But point where you might, what makes a place last or not, and what makes it die when it does, is, in the end, a more mysterious phenomenon. There is little method to the madness. A place is in vogue, or it is not. Sometimes it is, and then it isn't, and then it is again. And as with fashion, there is a weird kind of vicious circle involved with what's hot and what's not: People go to the places that are hot and they are hot because people go there. Pull the rug out from under either one, and it all just kind of collapses.

Yes, the strange thing is that whether a place lasts or not seems to have little to do with the place itself. The venue might remain much the same, same decor and funky beats and all, but the place, in the end, is only a husk—it is the beings within it that give it its soul. And so as soon as the crowd changes, so does the place. And in this city, crowds come and go like the wind.

Which is why each place is doomed from the very beginning. Because people in this scene are perpetually on the hunt for something new, something that will keep the night fresh, make it seem like our first time out, once again—and no one place can give us this forever. It will inevitably lose its pulse, fade into anonymity, disappear forgotten into the city night. And again, it has almost nothing to do with the place itself. It has to do with us, and the fact we always want the next best thing. . . .

The next best thing is not an easy thing to track down. You must seek it in the most random places and at the most absurd times. Of course, somehow this is part of the allure.

There is, for instance, that strangely exhilarating knowledge that by the time you actually go out, it's closing in on midnight, and everyone else—the parents and older folk, the cats who live normal lives, their patterns set, their eight hours of sleep essential—have already gone to bed. You are about to experience a part of life the routine-chained masses simply never will, striking off on your own secret path into the mysterious night. This all seems a matter of principle as much as anything else: After all, we could simply have some drinks after work, call it an early evening, but even though that might make a lot more sense, everyone can do that, and so who would want to? No, just as the places somehow mark us apart, so do the times we go there. It just wouldn't be cool to roll out any earlier. Yes, we are seeking not only the place but the time only the few will dare inhabit, we are exploring the Mariana Trench of the night, its deepest, most unknowable hours, and you kind of feel like a badass when you head out at such an illogical time: You feel, even if subconsciously, like you are on a mission, an elite band of Navy SEALs dressed in black ninja suits, hunting something down that is in a process of perpetual escape. . . .

Like some sort of yeti, or other mythical creature that may or may not actually exist, the coolest party seems to be in a constant state of retreat. It is always hiding, not only in space but in time. Thus it is that the best parties are often in strange, underground no-name dives instead of a super-posh place, or a posh place on a Tuesday instead of a Friday.

Ah, yes: Tuesday. Who would ever think of rocking it till six in the morning on a Tuesday? Exactly. There is a coolest night of the week here in New York, and it is the night that is least likely to hold that honor, the night when most would stay home, when only the hard-core dare venture out. This takes time to compute. When you first start hitting the town, it seems, of course, that Saturdays are the nights to rock it, 'cause everyone can and does, and Saturdays can be fun, for sure, no work tomorrow, etc., but then you begin to see that places are too hot and hectic and crowded, too many tourists and randoms, so you think maybe Friday is better, but it's pretty much the same, if not worse, and so then it is Thursday, which holds sway in a way and always will, the true start of the weekend in New York, because the next day is Friday, and all you have to do is struggle through it and then·it's the weekend, and so people celebrate, and yet it is quieter, not everyone is out, just some of us, just the slightly more adventurous and stupid, but then even Thursdays get old among those searching for something new, and so soon it is Wednesday, or Tuesday, that are the real cool nights to go out, the nights no one really knows about, the parties where no one and everyone will be. And then it is Monday that is the best, because who the hell would ever want to go out on a Monday? Sunday, for me, is sacred (a day devoted to recovery, I vow to do nothing but nothing on Sundays) but some, I believe, have even now decided that that day is best, too. Yes, we are always in search of the strangest, most inconvenient places and times in order to find the party that no one but anyone who's anyone knows about, burrowing the night like eager squirrels into secret corners, trying to make it our own, hiding it away from the masses until it's discovered and the elusive path of the coolest party in New York wanders on somewhere else, moves to another place, another time, looping back on itself, Monday swooping back to become Saturday, or Tuesday, or Thursday, always Thursday, Thursday, Thursday.

Or until the party becomes so secret, it simply disappears. Because that seems the logical conclusion to our strange search for the hidden party: as if the perfect place would actually be somewhere that had no one else there at all—just a big mirror hung up somewhere central to remind you of how cool you are that you and only you were in the know enough to find this spot.

## SOMEPLACE, ANYPLACE ELSE

There are, of course, more practical reasons we tend to get such a late start. For one thing, this is New York, and shit doesn't really get hopping till one in the morning or later, even on a Tuesday. Show up at a hotspot at eleven o'clock and it can feel like a seventh-grade dance—all these people standing around an empty dance floor with their timid faces, watching, waiting, drinking; they might as well be wringing their hands in embarrassed anticipation. You can feel naked if you show up too early at a joint, too exposed, no faceless bodies to disappear behind, your groove not on yet, your conversations awkward, your sips of your drink and your drags of your cigarette tentative, anxious. . . .

Of course, if you wait long enough, the night will begin, and it's funny how it happens, a gradual increase in volume and capacity, a gradual dimming of the lights and brightening of your buzz—because, in the end, the night begins around you when it begins within you—until it all reaches a threshold and something suddenly snaps, and you look around and the night has begun: People are throwing their heads back and laughing and their cocktails are tipping precariously and little gulps are spilling on the floor, and the music is louder and the dance floor is filling (always the brave, beautiful women come first, and then the men follow) and friends show up you didn't think would be there, and sometimes you don't even notice it, the night's final beginning, it just happens, and all of a sudden you're in the middle of it, unaware, just another part of a beast that is awaking, shaking the sleep from its hairy coat.

But though it can be an interesting study in anthropology to show up at a place too early and watch it find its rhythm, it's really not the move. Yes, it's no mystery why it's called "fashionably late"—it's simply too cool for school to roll in when the party's already in full swing, and this is what Zoo likes to do, being the cool cat he is: He likes nothing more than to show up at the right place at the right time. "Prime time," he calls it, which, depending on the night, falls somewhere between the hours of one and three. This, in the end, is the mission: to wind up at one of these ridiculous places at the very height of one of its ridiculous parties, and for the most part, Zoo has it down to a science.

The only problem is, since Zoo wouldn't be caught dead at a place too early, he sometimes overcompensates by going so far in the other direction that the party's almost over by the time we arrive. But Zoo has a schedule, even if it is a little skewed. He has to follow his routine, make his rounds, put in appearances, complete his night's circuit. Zoo, after all, is stubborn. He likes to do things the way he likes to do them, even if they don't make any sense.

Some of his ideas about space and time do make some sense, though. He would tell you, for instance, that if you show up at a place on time (i.e., late), you want to have that perfect buzz already kicking, so that even though you've just arrived at this party, you are nonetheless in sync with it, as if you have somehow been there all along. No, show up sober to a raging party and you'll feel out of place, separate, which can inspire bad judgment, like trying to catch up by drinking lots of shots quickly.

This is partly why you never start out where you want to end up. Your first stop of the night will be a pre-game joint, so-named because it is here that you will get your game going, your drink and groove on, and pass some time before the time comes to hit up the real spots. And so I guess that's what we're doing here at Lux: getting drunk and wasting time. But the fact remains that I'd rather be doing this at almost any other place. Yes, though Zoo loves this spot and the way they treat him, and despite the fact that Lux—or a place like it—is a necessary evil, more often than not, I find myself disappointed here. After all, beyond the waitresses, mostly an untouchable commodity, the women at Lux are nothing remarkable, and the rest of the crowd is drab and suited and tame. Yes, I am often struck, whether I'm at this stupid place or some other not-so-happening spot, by the obvious knowledge that there are better places to be.

This is a New York thing. In other towns and cities throughout the world, there is not always a better place to be. Out in the eastern Long Island summers, for instance, on a Thursday night, there is really only one club even open: Jet East. Now, this is a pretty good party, but it is nothing special—it is not the New York I have come to expect from a rocking night out. But it's what there is. You know from the moment you walk in there that unless you want to drive the two hours back into the city, this is as good as it's gonna get. And so here's the thing: It becomes enough. You resign yourself to it, to the merely pretty women, the never-quite-full dance floor, the mediocre beats. You have a couple drinks, chill with your good buddies on a couch, check out the scene, the girls, the funny things that happen. You are content, because you know there's nothing else that could be better. You know there's no other possibility—so you don't stress it.

Right now, if Lux were the only possibility, the only place to go, trust me, I'd have a good time here. But how can I when I know there's so much more out there, when I know without a doubt that there's a better place to be? Yes, though I should be wiser, I've somehow gotten sucked into the whole bullshit theory that it really does matter exactly where you go, and I look around me at Lux and see the lack of cool and want to get the fuck out. Knowing what the night offers, I want it all or nothing. I get bored at so-so spots, at dive bars and Irish pubs, do not like the skewed ratio of men to women, the bad eighties butt-rock from the jukebox. I shift from foot to foot like a pigeon, glance at my watch, finish my drinks quickly, want to fly away.

And it always seems that it's at times like these—when all I want is to get the fuck out, go someplace else, anyplace else, just go—that Zoo's actions take on an excruciating slowness. . . .

"Zoo, my man, let's get out of here." I have been waiting to leave Lux since I got here, and can take no more.

"What's your hurry, man?"

"Well, according to you, we have like fourteen more places to go, and it's getting late."

"Yo, dude, chill, man. Just let me finish my drink. We'll break out after this smoke. . . . Trust me, dude."

My groan is not entirely internal. No one takes longer to do simple things like drink their drink or smoke their smoke. And so he sparks a Camel with a cupped hand (we tend to ignore the recent smoking ban, and for the most part, it tends to ignore us) and proceeds to enjoy a twenty-minute butt. I don't know how he does it—it defies physics. Part of the problem is he spends a lot of time just sitting there with the cigarette at the end of his fingertips—simply chilling, nodding his head to the beat, looking off into the distance, enjoying the feeling of the thing in his hand— and it ends up smoldering more than burning, until he'll put it to his lips and take a drag and it lights up and sizzles and he exhales and nods and the cigarette returns to its near-dormant state, like the barely beating heart of a deep-sea creature, a thin wisp of smoke drifting up off the tip. And his drink, too—he relishes his omnipresent Sapphire tonic with a splash of grapefruit as if it were the last glass of water in an endless desert, taking such tiny, casual, infrequent sips of his cocktail that the ice melts and waters the thing down at the same pace that he drinks it, so that the level of the liquid never seems to actually diminish. And he has no clue how excruciating it can be, he is just doing his thing the strange way he does it, which just happens to often be at the wrong place in the wrong speed at the wrong time, not by any sort of malicious design on Zoo's part, but simply because that's the way he is.

And so here I am at Lux, literally cringing with discontent, shaking my head at Zoo and the blank enjoyment on his face and cursing him under my breath, wondering what the fuck we're doing here, pissed that Zoo made me come up here once again for this glaring lack of a good time, aware that above all I am wasting valuable moments in the always too-short night. It is at times like these, when Zoo might notice me steaming and glaring at him, that he will laugh—he has a disarming, infectious laugh—and give me a friendly punch in the shoulder and say something like,

"Dude, don't look so bummed out, man." And Zoo will take another tiny sip of his drink, another smooth drag of his smoke, and then say something like, "It's all in your perception of it, dude."

He's right, of course, the bastard. It does all depend on how you look at it. And this is the reality that's too easy to glance over with your eyes looking forward, onto the next: Things are fine here. I mean, shit, here I am sitting with one of my best friends in the world, we have a couple shots of chilled scotch warming our bellies, we're talking bullshit, nothing, work and women, smiling at the pretty waitresses as they pass, and it is the perfect start to the evening. Nothing so bad about any of this. And Zoo knows it.

I mean, just look at the guy: sipping so casually on his drink, nodding his head to the beat and just beginning to get his groove on, rapping shit with the bartender, hooking us a couple more free shots of chilled Dewar's . . . just taking it easy, enjoying the night and the way it's just getting started. Yes, for Zoo, this is simply the beginning, and yeah, we could be somewhere else that might be more bumping, but we will go there next, the night is young, and this is fine for now, this is perfect, just having a couple drinks in a mellow spot before we head out on the town. Look at Zoo, the way he takes himself so easy, seems so unconcerned, so imperturbable, so content with where he is and where he's going, no rush, everything will work out fine, he knows, and as much as it's infuriating, it's a lesson of its own: enjoying the moment, the smoke you're smoking, the taste of your drink, the shots slowly warming the belly and heart, the presence of a good friend. Being happy where you are. I mean, just look at him.

Look at me: my brow all furrowed and eyes flitting

about the room wanting anything but this and anywhere but here—a face of utter disbelief, like someone had just insulted my mother. And looking at myself for an instant through Zoo's eyes, I cannot help but laugh. It is a laughing matter, the sourpuss faces of disappointment people put on so unnecessarily in a night meant solely for enjoyment.

This is a very New York thing I'm doing, being discontent with where I am. It is a very New York look I have on my face, this scowl. In the city night, someone is always complaining about where they are, wanting to leave, head someplace else. *This place sucks, let's go, this place sucks, too, let's go, everywhere sucks, let's go.* No place is ever good enough.

Yes, we are New Yorkers, and we love creating our own little dramas and discontentments and reasons to brood. It gives us something to do. So it is that you will often see people looking bored at a place—beautiful women especially have perfected this look. The place itself seems irrelevant. Indeed, the more rocking the party, the cooler you are for looking bored there.

And, sure, there's something kind of fun about appearing uninterested in the midst of the most thrilling of environments, but it's far too easy to believe your own hype and forget it's all an act. It's far too easy to end up like me, some gloomy Florida bog steaming in the night, wishing for someplace, anyplace else.

Yes, the city night changes you, and not always for the better. Suddenly so concerned with being at the best possible place that you are never content with where you are— there's always someplace theoretically cooler—and so you skip from spot to spot, a tenseness in your shoulders, that flutter in your stomach that says *go go go,* and no matter where you get to, the search continues, because even when you arrive, you have to get into the VIP room, where it's really happening, and then the VIP room within the VIP room, and so on, and you can spend a whole night on your way somewhere, waiting in line after line to get in, and further in, and yet never arriving, never there. Because what you are seeking is by its very nature always some other place.

Or some other time.

And it's not that people don't feel true boredom at these places—after all, right now I really am bored shitless here at Lux—but the fact is, that restlessness, that urge to go, comes as much from within ourselves as it does from the place itself. Places get old and tired because people get old and tired, their eyes glazed over, jaded. Place is just the scapegoat. Again, as Zoo said, it's a matter of perception.

I think back to how I used to see the night when I first began going out. Just coming back to the city from high school or college and going out for a beer—it didn't matter where—just being out in the city night was enough. Even dive bars were palaces back then. And you knew you would end up somewhere crazy, this was New York, your home, and you were back with all your friends and you knew it would be a good night because it was already a good night, because when you are happy, no matter where you are is the best place to be.

Of course, I romanticize a bit, because these were the years when it did begin to matter where you went—Zoo was already starting to get hooked in—and there were suddenly such things as places to be: Spy Bar, where you could look down from the balcony with antique binoculars at the plush red couches and the beautiful models dancing on them, basketball players looming up from shadowy corners, magnums of champagne on the tables . . . Au Bar, Moomba, Life. But it did not yet matter to me. I was happy anywhere, I loved it all, but I admit I loved this new scene especially, it was a whole world I had never even imagined, and it was just crystal, it sparkled. I felt like I had entered Wonka's Chocolate Factory, and the look on my face those nights was one of washed-clean wonder.

And so I question sometimes if it is not so much a place we are seeking as it is a time. Maybe what we're really looking for is our old way of looking, the night as seen through our youthful eyes, open and endless and possible. Maybe, in the end, we're just out here looking to be young again.

Of course, the funny thing is, you never know—tonight could be one of those nights you will long for in the future. Nostalgia is forever based on now. You will yearn for this one day. . . .

## WHEN SPACE AND TIME UNITE

I know what the right thing to do is—to laugh at myself and all my mopery, all my ridiculous desires for things that disappear, or elude, or may or may not have existed in some indeterminate past. I know I should allow myself to be happy where I am, let go of that relentless urge to go. But I've also begun to recognize that such an urge has its uses.

After all, it is this desire for more that drives the night, and you out into it. I mean, if you were truly happy where you originally were, at home, why would you have even bothered stepping out the door? And if you were satisfied with that first spot, well, then, who knows what you would have missed at the next? Because this feeling that there is always a better place to be will feed the search, the bar-hopping, the endless motion of the night, it will make us leave Lux, finally, to head to some other place, where we will maybe only have one drink, because this scene really isn't all that, either—there could certainly be something better—and so off to the next spot, which *is* better—there are beautiful women here and fat beats—but is it really as good as it could be? And so we have two drinks there, maybe three, but then someone mentions that other spot, the one we haven't even been to yet, and off we go again into the night, space and time zipping by, 12:15, 12:40, 1:10, 1:35, hotel bars, hip lounges, one club and then the next. . . .

And who could deny the good fun that comes of such a relentless, ridiculous search? The excitement of going to the next place, of walking into a scene you cannot begin to imagine—maybe it's a twenty-foot Buddha smiling se-renely down on the pandemonium, or half-naked acrobats suspended in midair above the dance floor, or a mermaid gliding through a giant aquarium behind the bar—of chill-ing, ordering shots next to two beautiful strangers, turning and taking a loop through the madness, passing judgment on the place, anyway—somewhere else might still have something more—breaking out, going to the next spot. Exiting, leaving, strutting out, too cool for this shit, Zoo shaking the big hands of bouncers at the door, "Yeah, we might be back later," which is a lie. Back out there on the city streets in the fine spring air, swerving from one place to the next, pausing on a brownstone stoop so I can smoke a joint, music drifting out from dimly lit bars, the glow-ing women and city lights, hopping a cab, or, if there are many of us, maybe even a limo, the night teeming with packs of kids prowling the pavement and the bums shaking and rattling their cups and singing their monologues to God, the ubiquitous delis where we'll stop in for smokes and cash, outside of them bouquets of flowers and fresh fruit and the delivery boys sitting on crates . . . The feeling of going somewhere, of moving your feet, the feeling of being in this city of endless possibilities and movement, all of it pulsating around you. And this is why it sometimes feels so right, the going, because you are matching the pace, the freneticism of the city, because you are on your way somewhere, you are in motion, no time to be disappointed, the world is all ahead of you and it is filled with possibility. You are moving into the future, buzzing with the dream of whatever might be next, and of course you'll probably walk into the next joint and it'll be the same old shit, but that's okay, because there's always the next spot, and the one after that. There is always another place to go.

And I know what I'm about to say is contradictory, I know I said that this search for place is all illusion, but sometimes this endless discontentment with where you are drives you to a place where you cannot help but be content, a space and time that obliterates all sense of space and time. Sometimes you do find the party, the one you've been looking for, the one so bumping that all of a sudden there is nowhere else, no other place you would even consider wanting to be. It's out there, even now, the elusive party, the one that will put an end to all your seeking, a place so crackling with electricity and good-hearted havoc it burns all that jadedness and want and gloom from your eyes. And you will finally find yourself where you want to be—at the right place at the right time—and it will feel good.

Of course, once you get there, if you get there, the question then becomes—can you get in?

# 3

## *Getting In*

Speak swiftly and carry a big soft.

—KEN KESEY

**"I HOPE THERE'S A CROWD OUT FRONT,"** Zoo says as we near our final destination. "Heh, heh, heh—I love that shit."

Tonight Zoo is happy. As we pull up to the club, there is the full-on alien landing-pad scene at the door: spotlights shooting up into the night, flashing police cars double-parked, big men at red velvet ropes standing guard, along-side them strange-haired hipsters with their clipboards and little earpieces, and, forming a massive semicircle around it all, a crowd of some of the most beautiful people in the world all waving their hands and shouting out names and being very unbeautiful and wanting with every ounce of their will only one thing: in.

It's enough to make some strange part of you want to get inside, too—just the pure weight of all those people push-ing against the ropes, straining for the door. It pulls you toward it, almost like a black hole, except for one thing: Almost no one is disappearing into whatever parallel uni-verse awaits on the other side. Yes, there is a force at this magnetic door that both draws people in and pushes them away, almost as if the very fact no one is getting in is what makes everyone want to get in, makes this crowd sick with some ancient lust, makes them frenzied, hungry, savage.

This is not a benevolent scene. I think of foaming dogs straining at thick chains. Big, bared teeth. It's vicious out there. You get the sense that at any point, the thin shell of remaining civility could crack; indeed, were it not for the huge bouncers looming there with their tree-trunk arms crossed, the crowd might just make a rush for it, plow down the ropes and over the frail, hip doormen (an entirely different breed than the bouncer) and through the door. As it is, I have seen women in high heels help each other scale ten-foot walls, and distinguished gentlemen in suits sneak under bushes to gain admittance to a place. (I've climbed some fences and tunneled through some bushes myself.) I have seen arrogant assholes start up shouting matches with the doormen—"Do you know who I am?" I've seen fights break out, the bouncers' flattening response, blood pooling on cool concrete.

Now, most sane people, upon seeing such madness at the door, would turn around and say something like, "Jesus Christ. Look at that fucking line. Forget this, let's break out." Not Zoo. As we close the cab door behind us, he is clapping his hands together and saying, "Yeah, man, yeah, that's what I'm talking about, this is what I like to see." For Zoo, a crazy line outside is a sign of what's happening inside. It means that something absurd—and you cannot know exactly what until you pass through the gates—is going on in there.

But that's not the only reason Zoo likes a line. It takes a certain breed to flourish in such a setting, and Zoo is that breed. He relishes the challenge. He even likes the fact that he might have to throw his weight around—"Yeah, dude," he says, surveying the scene and rolling and loosening his shoulders like a boxer about to enter the ring, "we might just have to flex." Of course, Zoo doesn't mind having to show a little muscle to get into a place. It reaffirms his notion that he's the man.

Besides, what line would really concern you if you knew you didn't have to wait in it?

## THE WIZARDRY OF ZOO

There are lots of things the normal night owl can do to increase his chances of getting in to a place, and for the most part, Zoo does none of them. He reserves no tables (though we will most likely at one point or another end up sitting at one for free). His name is on no lists (lists are for suckers, is how he looks at it). Worst of all, he usually rolls with me and a bunch of other buddies (having a lot of beautiful women with you is like having a VIP card in your pocket, and too many guys a death sentence).

No, the only rules that Zoo feels actually apply to him are his own. He will not stand on line (instead, he'll bypass it and roll right up to the front of the ropes, which doormen generally hate). He never pays full price (usually something ridiculous like thirty bucks), and he considers reduced tickets "a compensation for insult." And whereas some might literally stand around for hours to gain admittance to a club, Zoo will wait no longer than the length of a cigarette, puffed on impatiently, before he'll flick the butt into the gutter and say something like, "Yo, fuck this, man. I'm too cool for this shit," and head off to someplace else where he will be treated the way he thinks he deserves, like royalty. For Zoo, these are all matters of principle.

You would think this attitude would work against him, but strangely it's what gets him in. The very fact that he so flagrantly flaunts the rules sets him apart, marks him as different. After all, you have to have balls to show up with four, five guys, maybe one or two straggling girls, expecting to gain admittance. But without a second thought, this is what Zoo does, night after night, and it almost always works.

The thing is, as far as Zoo's concerned, he's so money he doesn't need models, lists, tables—all that shit is beneath him—and it seems the very fact he believes it, knows it, exudes it, somehow makes it so. Zoo has always been a prime example of "If you believe it, it's true." It's almost the Jedi-mind shit—*You want me to come inside.* Indeed, he has such faith that the club will be better off with him in it— almost like *they* should actually be the ones paying *him*— that there's just no way they're not granting him access. It hardly matters whether he's at one of our haunts where the doormen have known him for years or some new joint he's never been. So it is that even in Las Vegas, Miami, London, his first time checking a club out, he still bypasses the line and walks right up to the front of the ropes like he's been a regular for years, and the doormen take note, come his direction, stick their hands out like they're not sure if they should know him or not. And Zoo gives them a firm handshake and a pat on the shoulder and a friendly grin and starts rapping his rap: "Yeah, man, I'm Zoo, man. What's your name again? Good to see you." And then there is the list of his nightlife contacts, brief and to the point: "Yeah,

I've worked with blah blah blah back in New York, and I know blah blah blah," and he establishes himself as someone connected, someone who belongs at this place, someone they should know, and the ropes open, and that is that.

Yes, Zoo's attitude is visible, tangible—even if the doormen don't know him, they respond to him. How could they not? Zoo is an anomaly at the door. I mean, just look at the guy: hip and dark and handsome, at home, at ease, content. Out amongst this frenzy of angry animals, people shoving and shouting out names and scowling and sneering like a pack of wild jackals, he is the only one really smiling, the only one truly unconcerned. He sticks out. He has *presence.*

And so when it's a night like tonight, and we're at one of our haunts where Zoo does know the doormen—forget about it—he's unstoppable. He bypasses the line, strides that long New York click of black shoe right up to the ropes, the doormen notice him, recognize him, smile back at him, the ropes part, Zoo shakes hands and kisses cheeks and gives everyone big friendly grins and pats on shoulders and he calls everyone by name, and then comp tickets are passed out and VIP bracelets and all the rest of it, and we roll right in.

You would think to get away with all this Zoo would have to be some sort celebrity or billionaire. He's not. And this is what makes his particular brand of magic so impressive. He's just Zoo. And somehow or other, that's enough.

### THE POLITICIAN

"Zoo, how the hell do you hook that shit?" I'll ask him, every now and then, after he's just pulled off some miracle like walking six dudes into one of the hottest clubs in New York.

"Yo, don't worry about it," is his reply. "You know how we do."

He probably wouldn't admit it, but Zoo's worked hard to attain such serenity at the door. It wasn't always this easy—Zoo and I have shouldered our fair share of rejections and denials, too. I can't count the times we've been dissed, glanced over, laughed at, ignored; we've heard the "Sorry, guys, can't do it, not tonight, not with no women," and worse, the lack of any explanation whatsoever, only at most a sideways glance like "Who the fuck do these guys think they are that they want to come through *this* door?" Even now some of the doormen we've known for years will still give us shit, just to fuck with us, and they'll shake their heads at us and grin and say, "Do you guys even know any girls?" or "Why don't you guys ever get a table?" or "When was the last time you guys paid full price?" But inevitably, the ropes will part, and they'll comp us, anyway.

The thing is, as far back as I can remember, Zoo's been working it, spending a hefty portion of each night out furthering his connections, establishing and reestablishing himself—and he just keeps getting better at it. He's made it his business to know everyone in the business, and, more important, to be known, and his years of networking have paid off: Zoo is now irreversibly hooked in. A glance through his cell phone would reveal the digits of the club scene's most powerful figures, the guys who literally rule the night not just in New York but across the world. And the strange thing is, for Zoo, all this networking is hardly conscious.

This is not an assumed affectation. This is Zoo. He's hardwired for these dealings. Yes, Zoo's a politician, a hustler—but not in any sort of malevolent way—just in the way he always seems to be in a constant state of working it. And he *loves* working it: meeting people, introducing himself, rapping the rap, establishing his presence, negotiating the night. It's just the way he is. Even when it can't possibly serve him any real purpose, say, on the laid-back Caribbean island of Tortola, where velvet ropes do not exist, still he's on the job, smoothing his ins with the bartenders of beach-shack bars: "Hey, man, it's Fritzy, right? Yeah, I'm Zoo, we met last year, good to see you. . . . So how's it goin' man, everything good with you? Good, good. So things just getting started in here or what?"

No, you couldn't stop Zoo from talking the talk even if you tried, it spills from him as natural as rain from the sky, and lucky for Zoo, it's an invaluable skill when it comes to navigating the night. "You got to have a smooth lip," is how he puts it. In other words, you need to know how to bullshit, to be completely comfortable rapping about absolutely nothing—the weather, the crowd, the night—with people you hardly know. Zoo does this like no one I've ever met.

Then there's his memory for names and faces—a politician's memory, uncanny at worst. Yes, like some sort of hip young ambassador to the night, he seems to know everyone, and everyone seems to know him: doormen he met more than ten years ago, back in the prime days of Au Bar and Spy Bar and Life, bartenders who'd just arrived in the city the week before, hostesses and owners and the hulking bouncers in the corners, and in a single night, he will make his rounds dutifully, greeting them all by name and shaking their hands and smiling and patting them on the shoulder and saying, "How are things, John, Emily, Pablo, Mark, Rich, Wass, Randy, Kiefer, King, good to see you. What do you think, not bad tonight, huh?"

And there is nothing insincere about it—that is his greatest charm. He really does want to know how things are, he really is glad to see them, he really does want to know what they think, and in a night so thick with insincerity, a guy like Zoo can be a welcome relief—his familiar antics, his familiar, friendly face, his interested, slang-laden voice, the fact he knows their names and they know his. And so there's a sense in which, for the moment they spend with Zoo, all of these stressed-out employees can quit their bouncing and bartending and working of the door, they can quit being at a job and just be people again, so sincere the Zoo is, and for a brief instant in this complicated night Zoo's easygoing presence somehow allows it to be just two people shooting the shit, everyday banter. And then he moves on to the next guy.

Yes, Zoo's great secret is not so much a conscious effort at networking as it is simply that he's a good kid. Sure, he's wise enough to know that remembering people's names and keeping up his rap with all the right folks will get him lots of perks—free drinks and comps and VIP bracelets—but there's still something amiable about him that manages to cut through all that.

In a night so filled with bullshit, this matters more than you might think. The thing is, as much as Zoo emanates confidence and certainty—and yes, even ego—his presence is never antagonistic. This is what truly sets Zoo apart from the rest of the people who try to bully their way into a joint. After all, it's a fine line between having an attitude like Zoo's and being an asshole. You don't, for instance, want to be so charged with ego and caught up in your own hype that you butt heads with the guys at the door, do battle. Do not try to pull rank on the doormen, make yourself out to be better than them. The fact is, outside a club, there is no one better than them. They are the gods of the doorway, its stone-faced gargoyle guardians, and you will not outrank them, you will not win a power struggle, and they will not take it lightly if you try. And so to puff yourself up all big and go chest to chest with these guys, looking down on them and acting like the shit, tossing out those birdlike cries of "I know so-and-so and so-and-so, I'm best friends with the owner," and the completely unrecommended "I could get you fired"—good luck—such pretenses do not sit well with these gentlemen at the door, especially if they're not even true. Making yourself out to be the big cheese, if you're not, only makes you stink, and these guys have the noses of wolves, and will sniff you right out. . . . "Oh, yeah? You're good friends with the owner? What's his daughter's name? Oh, really, you don't know? Well I guess you're not that good friends with him, then, huh?" Yes, no matter how cool or important you think you are, you are not so cool that you can afford to be an asshole. (Besides, there's no way you can out-asshole the assholes at the door. These guys are paid to play the part, and they play it well. With only a glance—or lack thereof—they can make you feel two feet tall.)

Which is why Zoo takes such an entirely different approach. He seems to know instinctively that these are battles that cannot be won, and so should never be begun. Sure, he might rap his rap a little bit, toss out a couple important names to establish who he is if necessary, but the manner in which he does so is first and foremost friendly. And he has such an easygoing bearing about him, it's disarming. From these men practiced in scowls, Zoo's positive, welcoming presence elicits smiles. Yes, this is what Zoo does: He treats these guys like human beings, and he gets treated like a human being in return.

The thing is, though their faux-fur coats and leather pants and glassily disinterested eyes might belie it, these doormen are of course people like the rest of us, just normal guys—folks not much older than kids—and they're part-time actors, or work days in some software company, and they're just doing their job, a tough one, an important one. And since this job is as much about denying the wrong people entrance as it is about letting the right people in, it breeds deep contempt. The crowd seethes with it. And sure, the occasional doorman might thrive on such hatred, revel in their position of power, but the truth is that for most of them, their favorite part of the night is not the ego boost of denying an asshole entrance, but the simpler things: throwing on a fine suit, sipping their first coffee of the night, hanging with the boys, seeing a familiar face. All the other shit—their sudden, shallow celebrity, everyone waving their arms at them and trying to get their attention and shouting out their names (and these poor bastards have heard their own names screamed at them so many times for so long now that you can see them literally cringe when they hear it shouted again)—all that crap they could do without. The simple fact is this guy is sick of being taken from, he's sick of people asking him for comps and VIP stamps, he's sick of everything about the night, and would welcome with great relief a note of sincerity from someone, anyone, something asked of him that does not require him to give. "How you doin, man? Everything good? You hangin' in there?" Zoo's tilted, familiar face crossed with interest and concern, his friendly hand on their shoulder, his politician's talent for making them feel like, for that moment, they're the only one in the world. Yes, just by being himself, Zoo has managed to turn these glowering figures of authority into friends. No longer is it patron and employee, but just two cats chilling in the night, both out in the cold.

## REJECTION

Me, I play a good sidekick, but that's about it. Without Zoo, I am mostly useless when it comes to getting into a place. The simple fact is I have few of the networking skills that exist so naturally in Zoo. I do not have the attitude, the confidence, the glow of certainty that hangs about him. I feel bad bypassing the line and walking right up to the ropes—after all, who the fuck am I to cut in front of all these other people? Zoo, on the other hand, is so sure of himself, no matter where he goes, that he even had no qualms using his Disney World VIP pass to cut in front of all the super-psyched little kids waiting eagerly for their first ride on Space Mountain. And talking the talk? Forget about it. While Zoo could talk a gypsy into selling him a rug for free, my rap is awkward as the chortle of a long-necked bird—I just can't do it, and feel far too self-conscious when I try. And as far as remembering names and faces, well, I can hardly recall ten of my friends' names, much less the vast network of promoters, owners, doormen, bouncers, bartenders, hostesses, and bar backs that Zoo knows cold as family. I just don't have the personality for it.

These are things I cannot really change, either. Sure, over the years my confidence has grown and my lip has smoothed and the Zoo within me has evolved, but the simple fact is I am not him, and as much as I love the guy, I would not want to be. Nor could I. The wizardry of Zoo is not something that can be affected; the results would only be transparent. The plain truth is that these are talents you either have or you don't, and if you don't, there's not a whole lot you can really do about it.

Almost all the methods for gaining admittance are similarly flawed in their logic. Sure, they seem simple enough: You want to get in—reserve a table, know someone at the door, roll up with six beautiful women draped across your shoulders like slender, furless coats. But if you don't have a cool grand-plus to waste on magnums of Cristal and six-hundred-dollar bottles of vodka, the table thing's out. And if you don't know anyone at the door, well, that's another impenetrable circle you find yourself outside of with no way in. As with job placement, it seems you need to know people to know people; to get where you want to be, you somehow need to be there already. And women, well, that truly sums up the viciousness of the whole admittance situation, a circle which can most easily be traced by the following conversation: "Sorry, guys, but you need girls to get in." "Yeah, but the thing is, we need to get in to get girls." And so on.

Yes, it seems that as with much of life, you're either in already or you're fucked. I'm a lucky son of a bitch knowing Zoo and being generally acquainted with his whole extended network of the night—in a sense, I'm in already— but there are most definitely times when I'm on my own at night, sans Zoo, that I find myself on the outside again. No smooth-talking New Yorker working his magic at my side. The doormen unfamiliar, their eyes a cold mixture of glass and disgust. And getting in is essentially up to awkward, scruffy old me.

And me, well, there's really only one skill I've found myself able to apply from Zoo's vast array. It's the simplest one, and unlike all the rest, anyone can apply it: Be friendly. Because though it'd be nice to have the quick lip and political canny of a cat like Zoo, you might be surprised how far just being a gentleman can get you. Bringing it down to a human level, smiling and introducing yourself to the people at the door, saying, "Hey, man, I'm Tap, what's your name? How you doin', John, you hanging in there? If you get a moment, we'd love to come inside, check it out. . . ." If you are genuine enough, the answer, surprisingly, is more often than not, "Sure, man, just give me a quick sec, let me see what I can do."

Yes, a certain good humor, positivity, empathy, and patience can be useful characteristics to reveal at the door. After all, these are the qualities no one out here is exhibiting—everyone else is in jackal mode—and so they will give you a presence of sorts. You'll stick out. As Zoo proves, just being yourself, the naturally good cat you are, is always the best way. It can help turn business into conversation, figures of authority into friends. And it can help get you in, too. After all, it is these people's jobs to let good people pass. It can help to remind them that you, too, are just a good kid out looking for a good time, not so different from them on their nights off.

Of course, don't get me wrong—my civilities don't always work. Sometimes I'll extend a gentlemanly hand and say, "Hi, I'm Tap, what's your name?" and they'll give me a sideways glance like I must be fucking nuts and my hand is plagued, and turn away, leaving me hanging.

No matter how good your rap or how many women you're with or how friendly and polite you are, there is always the possibility of rejection. Even a master of night-life negotiations like Zoo still gets dissed every now and then—the party inside a big one, close to past capacity, the doormen's eyes glancing over us, beside us, through us, in search of someone more important, more beautiful, more famous, just like back in the day when we did not know them at all. If there is eye contact, it will be short-lived, a brief shake of the head: "Nothing we can do for you tonight, Zoo. Sorry." And it never feels good.

It's too easy to become obsessed with the whole getting-in thing, especially when you're dealing with the possibility of rejection. Maybe it's all that ego out there, teetering on the edge of being confirmed or denied, that makes us defend it so savagely, but the instinct at this point is to do anything and everything to get in. In the past, I have resorted to terrible acts to gain admittance to a place. I have left friends waiting out in the cold because they wouldn't let us all in at once. I have mentioned my somewhat famous father's name and his recent death to get into a VIP room: "You know who my dad was, right?" While rejection stings, it does not compare to how sick such actions made me feel.

Getting in should never be an act of desperation. For one thing, that kind of frantic want is not attractive. Doormen will smell it on you, wrinkle their noses like you've stepped in something, pass you over. (Indeed, it's almost like you have to *not* care whether or not they let you in, and then they will.)

But there's a more important reason than this not to

obsess too much about all the nonsense at the door: If you take it personally, it can so easily sour a whole night. Yes, a bad experience at the ropes can swiftly ruin an evening out, if you let it. Even if you end up getting in, you'll be so on edge from all the bullshit that there's no way you'll have a good time, the rest of your night will be tinged with negativity: You'll feel the tenseness in your shoulders, your neck, your jaw.

And so these days, I try not to stress getting negated at the door. I try not to let the urge to get in overwhelm my night. It's not worth it. You do what you can do, what you're willing to do—for me, that means being a gentleman—and beyond that, fuck it. If they aren't open to it, well, someone else will be. Whatever happens, don't let the guy in the fur coat wearing shades out at night wreck your good time.

Besides, if you can't get in, really, who cares? You'll go some other night. . . . And that's the great thing about New York. You don't get into one place, you can always go to a thousand others.


**GETTING IN**

But I admit it: When it happens, and you're the man who made it happen, it really is a wonderful feeling. Because every now and then, it is, for whatever odd reason—maybe some magazine connection, maybe an old friend who happens to be promoting, maybe because I introduce myself to the guy at the door like we were both normal human beings—me, scruffy little old me with my goofy grin, that gets us into a place. And it is then that I feel the pleasure that Zoo must feel every time he hooks this shit up, an injection of importance, a swell of pride, a literal boost to the ego. Yes, though the reality is that none of this shit actually matters even a little bit, for that moment, you feel nonetheless like you're somebody, the center of the world. For that moment, as you stand there ushering your friends through the ropes, all those untouched comp tickets in your hand, the beast of the club inside awaiting you, the music growing louder as you follow them in, you feel like the fucking man. . . .

It is at times like these that I sometimes suspect that Zoo might almost like walking into a place more than actually being there.

## 4

*Being There*

Home is where I want to be, but I guess I'm already there.

—TALKING HEADS

**THERE'S NOTHING LIKE** the feeling you get when you push through the doors and the night finally hits you: that rush of music thumping and people dancing and lights flashing through the darkness. It's as if you have entered the cavern of a massive multicellular organism, every particle of it writhing and breathing and alive. Indeed, there's so much going on—everyone everywhere moving and the music pounding so loud you can feel the bass vibrate deep in your most internal organs—that there's no way to take it all in. All you can do is let it take you in. Yes, all you can really do is smile, shake your head, and let it wash over you, let the amoeba swallow you right up. And before you know it—it can happen in less than an instant—you are a part of the beast, bumping your head to the beat and making your way to the bar. This is what you've been waiting for. All that other shit—the decisions on where to go, the restless search, the getting in—all that is behind you. You have finally arrived. You are home.

Zoo is a happy man, too. Usually so cool and collected,

he leads the way with the energy of a Boy Scout, swerving through the crowd, clapping his hands and nodding his head and stepping to the music like a chicken, his wings dipping, and at the appropriate moment, he may even toss a pistol-shaped hand up in the air and thrust it to the beat like he's busting caps in someone's ass across the room. "Shots!" he says, turning back to me and grinning his big grin, and pushing his way to the front of the bar.

Zoo has convinced me in his wisdom that doing shots of chilled Dewar's scotch is a good idea. It's not. But because arguing with Zoo is generally a dead end, I have resigned myself to his system. And so that's the first thing we order when we get to the bar: two chilled shots of Dewar's, two ice waters, a beer for me, and a gin and tonic with a splash of grapefruit for Zoo. "Two shots of WHAT?" the bartenders ask (unless they know us already, which they often do), and the look on their face when we affirm that yes, we want two shots of scotch, is one of incredulity, of a resigned, "Okay, you asked for it. . . ."

I think Zoo picked up the habit in college, looking for a drink that packed some heat in those cold New England winters, but he continued the practice in New York. And they do pack a wallop—take a shot of chilled scotch and it's like getting slapped in the face, socked in your gut. You have to pound a glass of ice water just to stay on your feet. And so we stand there at the bar and watch the drink-doctors do their shake and dance—there is nothing like the artistry of a fine New York bartender, those swift, graceful circles, that perfected blur of silver and liquid and ice—and we pick up the result, two cold little glasses filled with golden pleasure, clink them, raise them to the gods, swallow them down.

And it is a breathless event, a regimented process: The ice water must be pounded immediately after the shot if you wish to survive, and yet even with the water, you can just barely keep it all down; sometimes the brunt of the shot makes your mouth involuntarily salivate, it shoots hot tendrils of energy out into your body and you literally have to punch the air so you won't explode (indeed, Zoo has been known at these times to clench his fists and focus the crazy energy of the Dewar's shots into a tight-lipped kamikaze cowboy yelp—"YEEAAOOO!"—followed by two or three precise kung fu blocks). But doing a shot when you first arrive at a place roots you, somehow. It puts you in the swing of the party, ensures your final melding into the environment. Look around you after you've knocked back your first or second, and you're finally where you want to be.

### THE PERCH

After the requisite shots, Zoo, panther that he is, has only one thing on his mind: finding a table, a perch from which to look things over. It is important to find yourself a home base, somewhere you and your crew can chill, wander off from, return to. Thankfully, the fact that Zoo and I do not have enough money to get a table and the mandatory thousand dollars' worth of booze doesn't seem to matter. Zoo in his ambassadorial ways usually manages to hook us a prime place to sit for free.

So, before I know it, he has smoothed his ins with the maître d' and we have a table on the second floor overlooking the edge, and we'll sit and make ourselves at home, or stand with drinks in hand and peer down at the dance floor below and check out the sea of people grooving.

This is when you finally have the chance to take things in, when you have a drink in your hand and have just lit up a smoke. This is when Zoo is at his happiest: ego large from having just slipped all the immutable rules of the night. Just look at him, elbows on the balcony railing, leaning over the edge nodding his head to the beat ever so slightly, smoking his ever-present smoke and sipping on his Sapphire tonic and surveying the scene like a king his property, approval in his self-satisfied eyes. "I love this shit," he says, and I nod in agreement.

Yes, this is when Zoo is at his most content. He has found his spot, his nook for the night, and except for perhaps a trip down to the front door to help a friend past the ropes, here he will stay. He need not venture out onto the dance floor (as I at one point will), he is willing to just let the night wash over him. He has done his work, getting us to this place, and now it is all about the satisfaction he has from simply being here, in this hottest and hippest of spots, the whole scene a reflection and confirmation of his own coolness, irrefutable proof that he's the man.

## THE SCENE

This is an absurd scene. Looking down from our perch to the main floor, for instance, I see so many people down there that I can't even zero in on one, it hurts to try—every now and then my eyes will alight on a beautiful woman, and I will strain to keep the golden apparition in focus, but it is never long before she blurs again and is swallowed back into the madness. No, there's too much happening to see any one thing, I just see it all, this great writhing beast, fed by the music, growing, pulsating, forming strange patterns that remind me of waves of grain blowing in the wind, circular, rhythmic, contracting and expanding, or perhaps of some great wildebeest migration, or antimigration, multidirectional, random, pointless—all those hundreds of animals down there milling about, trying to get somewhere and going nowhere fast.

But the thing is those are not heads of wheat down there or horned antelope in some haphazard migration, but people, hundreds and hundreds of real, live, breathing human beings—a fact almost impossible to comprehend, there are so many of them—and every now and then, looking down at them all from above, I cannot help but wonder: Who the fuck are they?

Zoo has a better eye for picking individuals out from the masses. He's always pointing out people I probably never would have noticed otherwise—friends sitting at a table in a far corner of the room, beautiful women dancing in the tangled middle of the madness, celebrities basked in shadows. (And whenever I doubt the validity of someone he's seen, he reminds me of his "hawk eyes": *Come on now, dude—I got twenty-fifteen vision, yo.*) Tonight, from up on our perch, for instance, he zeros in on this tall, stunning blonde 350 feet away, dancing on a couch in the VIP room, and says, "Dude, wife material, check it," and I say, "Where, dude, where?" and before I even spot her, he picks Natalie Portman from out of the masses and says, "Dude, Natalie Pibbly, dude, look," and I say, "Where, dude, where?" and he says, "Right there, you monkey, chilling with Hugh Grant," and I say, "Where, dude, where?" And Zoo shakes his head and reluctantly extends his arm and I follow the line of his pointed finger and there she is, standing next to

Hugh on a VIP banquette curled over laughing her little-girl laugh at some comment the lucky Brit bastard just made.

Who are these people? These are some of the most famous people in the world. Yes, there are times when it feels like celeb city in these places. Hilton sisters and other stunning little heiresses sprout like mushrooms from the velvet couches, the kids from *That 70's Show* roll in sporting their foam trucker's caps and shades, or Leo D. and his gang, New York Knicks and Rangers rear up from the shadows, the magician David Blaine materializes, offering to light people's smokes with a flame that appears in the bare palm of his hand, maybe P. Diddy is in the house, chilling at a booth guarded four deep by giants, or Jay-Z, and maybe later you'll end up taking a piss next to Bono in the men's room ("Bono, my man, I just wanted to say hello, I'm your biggest fan," and Bono glances over and says, "Well, maybe not my biggest fan.")

And down there, too, at the tables with the magnums of Cristal and the big bottles of Ketel One vodka and the cranberry and OJ mixers there are the heirs of Middle Eastern fortunes, the sons of art moguls and Wall Street barons, cool kids who are barely old enough to drink but are rolling like royalty anyway, and there are the promoters and club owners back there, too, chilling, the true kings of the night, surveying their creation with calculating, never-quite-satisfied eyes.

Then, of course, there are the women—they surround these men like lionesses after they've already had their fill of the kill, with a touch of disinterest. And these are not just women, but perfect specimens of the female form, they have legs that go on like parallel lines, forever, and breasts that need no bras, the nips perking through thin wisps of whatever clings to them, and fine smooth backs they show off with backless dresses, and faces so perfect that makeup would only be an insult, all lips and smoking eyes, and they are the kind of women that make you shake your head in astonishment, so stunning they stop hearts the way Medusa turned men to stone, with hardly a glance, and they're down there, chilling in the raised VIP area smoking cigarettes with practiced puffs and dancing with each other on the banquettes and throwing their slender arms in the air, devastating everyone and loving every minute of it.

But though the models and celebs and VIP lurkers might be the easiest to spot, there is of course every other kind of person down there, too. There are NYU and FIT and Columbia students out for a night on the town, there are high-school kids with fake IDs who aren't even old enough to smoke, there is the ancient man with the thick white mustache and the baseball cap whose shoulders the years have bent creaking toward the floor but who always seems to be out anyway, rocking it like he's twenty. In one corner, a girl is standing on a chair shaking a pink balloon to the beat like it's a maraca; on the dance floor some dude wearing big shades and a silver Afro is doing the robot. There are jacked guys with short spiked hair and striped button-downs, there are rail-thin hipsters in jeans and boots and faded T-shirts, there are Europeans and South Americans, sharp men with too-smooth accents and suits, there are girls fresh in from Kansas, Ohio, Nebraska, innocent as wheat.

There is everyone down there, each one an equally improbable existence, and a true list would be a near-infinite undertaking, which is why it can be overwhelming at times, sublime almost, to try to take it all in. But there are people you recognize, too, which helps. Yes, out in the middle of all this madness, this sea of strangers, an old familiar face can be such a sweet relief, it really can. It can even be enough to make your night, bumping into someone you know and who knows you—and it's not just the simple pleasure of seeing an old friend, though that would be enough—it's like it gives meaning to what you're doing out here. It makes you feel like you are a part of something bigger, like this is a journey you've been taking not alone but in good company, ancient friends traveling the same offbeat path.

And the night is full of familiar faces, thank God. New York is a small city: It rotates in quick circles. Out at night, I bump into girls I first knew way back in seventh grade, when we would French-kiss in the back of taxis. I see my best friend from when I was six, when we gleefully poured the entire contents of his parents' liquor cabinet out of his tree house. I see girls I have crushes on or who have crushes on me, I see girls I have dated or whom my friends have dated or who are friends with girls I dated, I see friends, and friends of friends, and friends of friends of friends of friends. I exchange pleasantries with guys I've known off and on for years but whose names, for some reason, I cannot for the life of me ever remember. There are others I pass by who I know I know and who seem to know me, but nothing will be said, 'cause neither of us can figure it out. There are those I think I know but do not, cases of mistaken identity: *Oh, sorry, man, I thought you were someone else.*

Then again, maybe you do know these people, somehow. The degree of separation in these clubs, after all, seems two at most. Because everyone is in their circles of friends and someone from each circle knows at least one person from the next and like some honeycomb it all goes on to infinity, so that if you live in this city night and frequent the same spots, there is no one you do not know, in the end.

This is part of what feels comfortable about the night. In one way or another, you are amongst people you know, and who know you. You are amongst people who are just like you: not necessarily in their skin color or background or anything like that, but in their simple belief in the night. They are out here on the same mission as you—to have a good time—and this is somehow enough.

This is not your usual New York. This is different. There are moments when it feels like you could look at almost anyone around you and nod. People forget themselves enough to open up to strangers. People connect. There are friendly, knowing grins amongst men who have never met. Women banter amiably to other strange women in the bathrooms. This is how it can be, the night, the party, the mission, binding you together. After all, here we all are, going through the same shit side by side. . . .

And so who the fuck are these people? These people are everyone, these people are you, these people are me. These people are no one. Yes, in a place like this, there's a wonderful sense in which no one is anyone anymore. Oh, we all do our best to be individuals—that's why we spend far too long dressing up or down or whatever—that's why I toss on that ratty baby-blue corduroy blazer and the fatly knotted tie and do not brush my hair, trying my best to affect a manicured dishevelment that will somehow set me apart. That's why that model is wearing the Page Six Six Six shirt or the tank top that says WILL FUCK FOR COKE. That's why that guy is wearing leather pants. That's why everyone paints these expressions on their faces, scowls and indifferences to mark them as above it all, separate, better. But the fact is, in a place like this, and as with most mass efforts at individuality, everyone ends up looking much the same, anyway. After all, it is dark in here, and in the flashes of light you catch only glimpses of appearances before they fade again into sweet, shadowed anonymity. Even the celebrities disappear into the dark and madness. Yes, it doesn't matter who you are, come to a place like this and you become a part of something bigger, a part of the party, a part of the beast. And it is a wonderful feeling. For the hour or two you spend here, you are connected to everyone else, drinking the same poison, feeling the same effects, moved by the same beats, tilting and laughing and dancing together, washed away. You are smaller and bigger all at once. In this big, dark, lonely city, you are, for once, part of a community.

## THE ARRIVAL OF THE CREATURES

Of course, community always begins and ends with your own little circle, the cats sitting at your table. Tonight, right now, it's just Zoo and I, which is the way it is a lot of nights. But I don't mean to belittle this. The truth is, I'm lucky to have the Zoo at my side.

Hustler, player, crafty ambassador to the night, Zoo is first and foremost a friend. I am too tough on Zoo, I suspect. I guess he's just an easy target—anyone who enjoys this crap as much as we do is. But you must understand that beneath the hip, hustling persona is a really good kid. As unpunctual as he tends to be, if it's ever anything important, he's always there in an instant. Yes, unlikely as it might seem, you can count on Zoo. He is thoughtful—he's always the one who's there to help me set up for parties, and to clean up afterward. And when he stays with my mom and me on Long Island for weekends, he brings her housewarming gifts, which he certainly doesn't need to: Tiffany candy bowls, multi-option showerheads that may or may not actually work; and he gives me birthday presents, too, which is also unnecessary: a leather Dopp kit, a classic wooden-handled switchblade he had to order from Italy. It's hard to imagine such kindness blanketed by all that coolness, but it's there. He is a good friend, and though he would probably never express it in words—*It's just really not his thing, dude*—he's got a lot of love in him, the guy.

All my friends do. It's hard to realize, sometimes—after all, I've known them for so long their presence seems a given—but they're all such good people, they really are. The day my father died, a lot of my buddies dropped everything to be there for me. They left work, canceled appointments. That night, my oldest friend, G, skipped his own engagement party to be at my side. And all of them said the same thing: "I know it doesn't need to be said, man . . ." and then they would trail off. And it didn't need to be said. Their mere presence was more than enough.

So it is with the night. Having good friends at your side, it's enough, it's more than enough—it's what it's all about. Just having Zoo as my wingman would more than suffice, and often does. But the great nights remain the ones when we all end up together, the old gang reunited.

Maybe it's just because I stay out of the planning process, and therefore am never quite aware of who's doing what where, but I am always surprised—indeed, I find it almost absurd—that our crew manages to find each other in the night. I mean, of all the places to go in the city, the chance that we would all end up at the same club; and further, that out of the five hundred people packed in this place, these guys would somehow be able to sniff out the Zoo and me, tucked away at our little table upstairs. But again and again it happens. One of those big nights in the city, all of us out and about for one reason or another, doing different things, something will pull us together. We will coalesce, without even really meaning to, almost like muscle memory. (We have, after all, been doing this shit for quite some time now; raging together in the New York night is engrained in us bone deep.) Yes, these days, it's not so much good planning as it is a strange sort of gravity that brings us all to the same place at the same time, a kind of heavy liquid metal in our respective guts that can only be at true rest when surrounded by itself.

So here I am with my good, good friend the Zoo, perched above it all, a part of it all, closing my eyes and dancing and breathing in the sweet electricity of this strange, frenetic beast of the party, when from behind me I hear a "Mraa!" and turn to find that Stibbs has shown up, rolling in casually with his backwards baseball cap and loose-fitting, untucked linen shirt, the benevolent smile beneath the cherubic curls, a twelve-year-old scotch in one hand and in the other, a cell phone/iPod/mini-mega-computer, the latest. Stibbs and I have been rocking it since we were teenagers, when he used to roll out at night to all the Hampton hotspots wearing flip-flops and his "Fletch" Lakers basketball jersey, a two-day beard coming in, looking more money than anyone else because even in rags the velvet ropes somehow always swept right open for him.

And right behind Stibbs is Fatdog, dressed impeccably

in a tailored suit and his hair slicked just so, and he's got this big mischievous puppy-dog grin spread across his mug and two lovely little nymphettes in tow, and he proclaims, with great joy, "BACAAW!" Good-hearted, smooth-talking, banker turned actor turned banker, the Fatdog is a species of his own. Part man, mostly puppy dog, and all instinct, Fatty always seems to be rooting around and digging himself into or out of some mischief or other—as a result, the look on his almost boyish face consistently pleads guilty and innocent at once.

And me, well, when greeted by such monsters, I try to respond in the appropriate ways: with big grins, giant bear hugs, several big open-palmed thwacks on the back. Or perhaps it is the stylized handshake, our palms coming together with a great pop, the maneuvering of wrists, and then the final satisfying snap of fingers or pound of fist. Maybe it's just a simple understated nod of the head. And we say:

"Hey, what's up, man, how's it goin?"

"Good, man, good. What's up with you?"

Or maybe we simply say again, "Mraa!" the yelp of a baby dinosaur, or a wayward extinct bird, the dodo, perhaps, to which there is no more appropriate reply than a similar one—"Bacaw!" (Yes, my friends and I, as with all true friends, are beyond base communication. We have gotten to the point where the raising of an eyebrow, a mischievous grin, the absurd cry of an ostrich speaks more than well-versed diction ever could.)

And Fatdog will introduce Zoo and Stibbs and me to his little friends, and whisper in my ear, "Tap, dude, the blonde, man, she's ready to go," and we will kiss their cheeks and they will kiss ours and we will say, "Hey, how's it goin', good to meet you," and promptly forget their names.

And we will crowd into the table and we will chatter and there will be drinks and shots, but this is just the beginning. More creatures are undoubtedly on their way. With the addition of Stibbs and Fatty, after all, our sphere has expanded, its gravity grown stronger, its pull now inevitable. So that, not much later, G and Benny will show up together, two big beasts I've known almost my whole life, and G, in from the suburbs for a rare night on the town, is swaying and growling and his eyes are slightly glazed and even though earlier in the night he was complaining about coming to exactly this kind of scene, here he is anyway, gravity at work, having the time of his life, giving me a big hug and sloppy kiss on the cheek and saying, "I love you, brother." A polar bear in heart and body, full of loyalty and brawn, happiest when surrounded by snow, good friends, fish, G is bearish in mind as well. When things don't go as he planned (and G has a cruise-director complex, he's an obsessive planner), he will sometimes emit a low, guttural growl, and bypassing debate, resort immediately to brute force, manhandling naysayers around him into submission. Benny, a former comedian, martial arts badass, and self-proclaimed "pimp," mafioso-tough and brimming with a bravado that hides his big, romantic's heart from all but the closest of his friends, takes an alternate route upon arrival—from the very start he is talking shit and cracking jokes and calling us all dirty sluts: "Aw, you hooked up with her, Tap? I'm disappointed in you. Bitch went down on everything but the *Titanic*. . . ."

As I'm shaking my head at Benny, I'm bumped from

behind and turn, and right up in my mug from out of no-where is the Tako, hopping up and down with his chest puffed out like he wants to start a fight, theatrical madness in his eyes, shouting, "Damn, player, you ready to get your club on, yo! Huh? Huh?" Hollywood in his blood, Tako alternates between a completely normal, curious, polite young man and a rabid creature of randomness and lunacy, sporting strange Croatian accents for no particular reason, or howling out Japanese curse words he picked up on his travels like a mad coyote at the moon—*Ta-kohhh!!!*

Then my roommate, Hobbes, lanky and a realist like the wily cartoon tiger, rolls up with his Puma sneaks and Diesel jeans, his understated grin and wry, sideways com-ments—"So, here we all are again. Great." Hobbes and I grew up playing tennis at summer camp, and he's still the same good friend he was at eight, only now he's also a hip-ster, artist, and heartbreaker: the collection of photography and old-school sneakers, the quiet, mysterious good looks, the ruins of beautiful women left reluctantly in his wake. And right behind Hobbes is Whitey—the two of them have spent the night in some dive over by the Hudson, shooting stick and feasting on ribs and beer. (I think Benny was the one who came up with the nickname "Whitey," but it's ap-propriate. "I'm really white—it sucks," I heard the poor guy admit once, though beneath the perfectly parted blond hair, he's got more soul than most.)

And then, a little later, Big M—broad-shouldered and large with spirit, teddy bear crossed with Labrador, the eyes on his friendly, bearded face capable of mournfulness and silliness both (Hobbes and I once saw him make a girl laugh so hard she peed in her pants)—he shows up with his whole crew, which always seems to include several cheeky foreigners and at least two beautiful women who are in love with him, and before you know it we are all a big rollicking group, standing around and bullshitting and checking out the scene and elbowing each other and nodding and laughing, and this is my community, this is my circle, this group of howling dogs.

And I've known these guys for so long now—some of them from birth, some from grade school or camp in the summers, some from high school, and they've all known each other forever, too—that it's easy to forget how blessed I am to have these crazy bastards as my companions, to have roots that run so deep. Yes, I do not think I would have lasted so long in this vicious city, this bitch of a night, were it not for the fact that I've had my friends alongside me for the journey.

Not many people have this. New York, after all, is filled with people who have just moved here, who face these nights alone, and if not alone, then with a loose-knit weave of new friends that, no matter how well-meaning, are never quite the same as old ones. No, I do not envy the newcomer to this big city. It is a hard place to find anyone who will really open up, let you in. It is a hard place to get beneath the surface if you do not have those deeper connections there already.

And this old and trusted crew of mine, well, despite our sturdy roots, even we don't rock it like we used to, especially when it comes to the night. Yes, even this little community is dissipating. Shit, it's hard enough to get the guys together for a game of poker, much less a night out on the town, all of us raging together, the way it used to be. Because you could count on it back then—a big group of us, coalescing in the night, prowling the city streets and clubs together, stirring up trouble and good times. The night was our haunt back then. These were familiar grounds for scoundrels like us. But not so much anymore. The nights we all see each other, nights like tonight, they're getting fewer and farther between. Maybe it's just that a lot of these crazy cats are growing up: getting serious with their jobs and women, their health and sanity. G lives in the suburbs, has a house, a wife, a dog named Hunter. Stibbs and Whitey are engaged, can no longer partake in the enticements of the night. Hobbes and Fatdog are moving up their respective corporate ladders, can't afford to show up at work all hung over and shaking. People are quitting smoking, drinking, drugging. Usually these nights it's just Zoo and I out on the town, maybe the Tako thrown in for a little madness and good measure.

Of course, though the years may drift us apart, it hardly matters: When a night like tonight brings us together, we always pick up right where we left off.


## THE ART OF DOING NOTHING

And so now that we're all here, what do we do? What the hell does anyone do at these joints?

Not a whole hell of a lot.

Yes, every now and then, when the next day comes and someone asks me what I did the night before, I will answer, honestly, "Not much."

Of course, this isn't to say that crazy shit doesn't happen every now and then. It does. Like the time Fatdog got beat up by the buffed lesbian for making moves on her slender femme partner (Fatdog is always sniffing out some kind of trouble or other); or the time my friend Jimmy decided to whip it out in the middle of the outdoor VIP room of Southampton's posh nightclub Tavern and take a piss right there on the fake green Astro-grass, an act so outlandishly obvious, no one even dared notice but us. But such "events," if they can be called that, are the exceptions.

Yes, for the most part, not much is what will happen, and not much is what we will do. We will stand around and smoke too many cigarettes, one after the next. We will tap our feet, nod our heads, drum our fingers to the beat. We will sip on drinks, swirl the ice, stare out at the night, watch the madness whirl by. G and Benny and I will start up a little kung fu scuffle, until Stibbs notices a nearby bouncer getting edgy and settles us down. Hobbes will whisper something wry to Big M just as he's taking a sip of his cocktail, and the result is that, trying not to snarf, M projects the mouthful in a perfect, arcing fountain-spout four feet across the room, where it strikes me on my pant leg. We will all laugh. A good funky song will come on, and Fatdog finds an empty space to dance near the table, swings one of his nymphettes around like she's a rag doll, ends up knocking her head into some Swedish guy's shoulder, but no one gets too upset. To settle everyone down, Zoo will order shots from the beautiful half-Asian waitress and she will sashay off and return with a steaming cold tray of assorted drinks, and we will all raise our glasses, and Tako, madman that he is, will shout out nonsense Japanese idioms—*Nandayo! Konoyaro! Tabako! Tako!*—which when literally translated would make no sense—*What the fuck! Asshole! Cigarette! Octopus!*—phrases that if uttered in Tokyo would be fighting words and would probably get our throats cut by some fiery yakuza, but here in the New York night just mean, *Cheers, you crazy bastards, cheers*. And we will all shout and whistle and roar our own nonsense idioms in return, and raise our glasses, and down their contents, and our faces will contort and cringe, and we will shake off the shots the way dogs shiver off the sea, and there will be murmurs of "Goddamn!" and "I didn't need that," and Zoo will do his kung fu cowboy yelp "YEEE-AAOO!" and karate-chop the air. But G was in the bathroom, and when he returns to find that we have done a shot without him he will say, "What the fuck, dudes," and swaying and growling, force Zoo to order up another round, and Stibbs will say, "No, no more shots, *please*," but G won't take no for an answer—there is no way to deny those wild fiery eyes tilted with madness and drink, that low, guttural growl that could only emerge from the lungs of a polar bear. And so Stibbs will resign himself to the motion and return his gaze to the glow of his mini-mega computer, and when the shots come we will all down them anyway, raising our tipsy glasses to the gods. It seems we are always resigning ourselves to madness of one kind or another—after all, you cannot deny such rituals amongst good friends. It's simply not done. Besides, if it's not G, it's someone else, Zoo maybe, or Hobbes or Stibbs, or me myself, forcing us on toward oblivion. And who are any of us to refuse?

And so one of these wiseasses will say, "Why don't you roll up a doob, dude? I think it's your turn." And shaking my head semi-reluctantly, I will comply—sit myself down at our table and, keeping it low, twist up a fine spliff, Spanish-style, which when complete will be passed around, toked on leisurely, tilt us further into whatever plane we're trying for and will soon surpass, that place, wherever it is, we're going.

Even though, again, we're not actually going anywhere.

After all, these activities—drinking, smoking, getting high—are passive, static. We may be moving somewhere in mind, on toward oblivion, but except for the occasional loop or trip to the bathroom, our feet stay right where they are. We stand around, or sit, and tap our toes. We nod our heads to the beat, lean over the balcony with cold beers in our hands, take swills, puff on smokes, check out the scene from our perch, turn to each other to point out something we see, have brief conversations of little import.

And you might think that considering the fact we're not even really doing anything, we would at least have real discussions, but the truth of the matter is even those are few and far between. No, this is not the place for talking, for connecting in any deep and meaningful fashion—after all, it's near impossible to hear anyone anyway, what with the thumping of the beats. So it is that the majority of our conversations skirt only the very surface of things—music, drugs, sex, the absurd ass on the hot thing that just walked by, the fact we're probably all going to hell. . . . Even serious topics are swiftly dealt with by absurdities and half-wit: *war* ("Oh, man, that shit solves nothing," I say to Benny, who's on a tirade about Iraq, and he replies, all bravado, "It would if we just nuked 'em all"); *women* ("I don't even know what I'm looking for anymore," I say, and Fatdog says, "No one does," and Hobbes chimes in, deadpan, "I'm just looking for a nice piece of ass"); *astrophysics* ("You've heard the theory there's a black hole at the center of the galaxy, right?" I ask, and Stibbs replies, "You *are* a black hole at the center of the galaxy").

What do we talk about out there in the night? Everything. Nothing. But mostly nothing. We'll turn around and bump into each other—the night is full of this pinball interaction, bumping into one person and chatting briefly and then turning and veering off once again till we collide into the next person—and we will grin big grins and pat each other on the shoulders and though we've already covered this territory, we will say things like, "So what's going on, man?"

"Not much, man, not much. What's going on with you?"

"Not a whole lot. So things are good with you?"

"Things are good, dude, things are good."

Sometimes the banalities get mixed up: "So what's up?"

"Good, man, good. How are you?"

"Not much."

But the words are just words, rituals, and it is a rare thing indeed for a question to be a true question, or for an answer to be a true answer. You do not hear, "Things are not good, man, things are not good at all," even if that's the way they really are: bad. No, we are men, and this is the night. The only acceptable interaction is practiced bullshitting, wry remarks, laughter.

But the thing is, there's no fooling your good friends, so that when you reply, as you are supposed to, "Good, man, good," if you didn't actually mean it, they will look into your eyes and know what you really meant, and because there is nothing that could be said that would mean any more, all they do is nod and say, "Let's do a shot," but in that nod and those familiar, understanding eyes, there is all the solid ground you ever needed and ever will.

Yes, we are the best of friends already, and nothing really need be said to prove it. And so what could be more perfect for people who don't need to say anything to each other than a place where you couldn't say anything even if you tried? After all, you've known these guys since you were wearing Superman costumes and Jams, you've been through some *times* with these crazy bastards, some serious adventures, and here you are again, out on another adventure, out in your element, women everywhere and the music hot and bumping, the room tilting and swaying and this giant beast of a party swallowing you up and spitting you out, and you and your buddies need only look at each other and nod, this is it, you are with your best of friends rocking it together, grooving on the crazy night, and they're right there with you, feeling what you're feeling and seeing what you're seeing and knowing what you know, and you are kings, brothers, knights crowded 'round the same old couch and table, doing the same old shit.

And the fact we're doing the same old thing—in other words, not a whole hell of a lot—well, it's not as dull as it might sound. The simple fact is we don't need to do much. Just chilling here is enough. It is more than enough. Of course, part of the reason we can get away with doing so very little is that there really is so very much to look at. A good party provides endless visual and auditory entertainment. No matter where you turn, there is something, especially if you are men in love with women, like us. We could stand here all night and do nothing but watch the women drift by, feel our hearts swell and deflate like lungs. . . . There, the effortless glide of slender waitresses in black; there, swaying hips sashaying by; there, smoky, sex-singed eyes and spiked black hair; there, trim-bodied go-go dancers descending from the ceilings on twirling ropes; there, the longest legs you've ever seen, the shortest skirt. And it's not just the women, it's everything, it's the giant beast of the party, all around you, the endless bustle, people swaying and stumbling and spilling their cocktails and laughing, the busboys rattling by laden with their big plastic cartons of empty glasses, the music thumping and the conga drummers drumming and everyone hooting and hollering and hopping about and dancing, the hundreds of heads bopping and everywhere limbs, golden legs intertwined and arms tossed this way and that, throwing back shots and puffing on cigarettes and waving to the beat, a thousand-armed Indian goddess dancing the night into existence. Yes, there is an energy created at a good club, something not in any one thing, but in everything, in the air, electric, almost, and if you are in tune with it, you really don't need to actually "do" much at all to be in the best of moods, have the best of times. I'm not sure it even has to do with the drugs or the alcohol. At 2:40 in the morning, the height of a good party, you are feeding off something subtler, drinking the frenetic air itself.

And it feels good to not have to do anything, to be content where we are, here, now, together. After all, it is simple companionship we require and only that, and this is what we have—we are all here experiencing this thing, like teenagers on a couch watching a movie, or old men sitting on a stoop on a fine spring day, watching the world pass by, every now and then turning to each other to toss out a wry remark and chuckle.

Yes, it turns out that all we've really done by coming to this place is moved from one couch to the next. A different kind of motion picture before us. And it's kind of absurd. I mean, all of that motivation and the dressing up and the cab rides and the madness at the door and all the rest of it for *this?* All that just to sit around and check things out and bullshit over ten-dollar beers?

Apparently, yes. And I love it. As absurd as it may sound,

it's worth it, somehow. We spend so much of our lives doing, and right now, for once, we're just chilling, kicked back, letting things happen, watching the grand act of the night play itself out before us.

And there really is something amazing about being in a place where nothing need be said or done. It signifies the height of a good party, the height of good friends. It signifies true contentment, too, the way top-notch food brings silence to the dinner table, everyone munching away.

So it is that though we may not do much, or say much, these truly are the best of times. Because it's not so much what we do, in the end, that matters, it's how we feel, and we're feeling pretty good now, almost invincible, the warmth of liquor and ganja and good friends, big smiles coming across faces flushed and glowing. That simple sense of well-being. No rush, no hurry, happy where we are, here, at home. Yes, these are the best of times, nothing done, nothing need be done, nothing said, nothing need be said. Satisfaction.

Because the night can so easily go another way—everyone perpetually off to somewhere else, to the next club, or the one after that, or to the bathroom for another bump of *yayo,* and then back to the table to squawk on like a manic parrot and then off to the bathroom again, and when the bumps run low, it's all about getting more, dialing beeper numbers and exiting the club to wait for some drug dealer who may never arrive, and the whole night just gets fucked. Whereas it's a pretty good bet that when you've finally settled in and are all just chilling, not actually doing much, just sitting around, bullshitting, drinking, checking out the scene, kicking it with the kids, enjoying the moment, the company, well, even though you may not remember these moments too clearly in the future—after all, not a whole hell of a lot is happening to remember—nonetheless there's little doubt that at times like these, life is good. . . .

## INTO THE MADNESS

But every now and then, you find yourself aware of the complete and utter absurdity of the situation—this great rush of a good party pumping through your veins, through everyone's veins, all these people enjoying themselves, for once—and if you did not show your appreciation in some way, if you did not toss out a little kamikaze yelp of your own, or if you did not turn suddenly and with mischief in your eye shout to the waitress, "Shots!" or if you did not rise from the table and begin to dance, you would explode. You feel so good you turn and sock Hobbes in the shoulder for no apparent reason.

"Ow, dude, what the fuck?"

"Sorry."

Yes, in the end, I am not content just watching from the edge, as Zoo is. I feel the ancient need to lose myself in the thick of the madness, the heart of the party. I find myself wandering away from my friends, returning again and again to the balcony to overlook the crowd below, staring wistfully out over the scene, wondering what else might be down there. Because what I see down there—that boiling sea of madness—it calls to me. Yes, though I love my friends and the comfortable interactions we have, I feel the need for something deeper, something more. Something I can only find on my own. Because when you leave the safety of your little group of friends, the night becomes a different place: bigger, darker. You are a little vessel in a stormy sea. There is more potential for disaster and enlightenment both. Yes, I am a fool, and though all I ever needed is right at my table, these good times with good friends, I refuse to believe it, I venture off again anyway, and leave my crew behind.

Because though there's something empowering about being a regular in the most irregular of spots, fully at ease, calmly watching the madness go by, there are times when I just can't keep the cool composure anymore. Moments when it all becomes too much, the contrast too absurd, and I am projected from stillness into action, shot out of the easy orbit of my circle of friends and into the chaos of the night. And then there I am, off on my own, swerving through the crowd, prowling the madness, seeking out a prime place to dance.

**5**

*Into the Dark*

**RIGHT NOW IT'S NEARING** three in the morning, and I'm feeling pretty good. The night is at its deepest hour and the tunes are bumping and the air is electric, and I am doing what I feel I must do every night I go out, at least for a little: I am making my way to the center of the dance floor, the heart of the madness, to dance.

This is not as simple as it sounds. It is no easy thing making your way anywhere in one of these places. On the main floor, people are packed as close together as doomed Texas cattle, flank to flank, everyone moaning and groaning and exhaling hot, bothered puffs of air through flared nostrils, and trying to push their way somewhere different—the bar, the bathroom, the dance floor, the door. If you're not careful, you can get swept up into the wrong current and have no control over where you go at all. Mashed shoulder to shoulder, surrounded on all sides, you go where the stampede goes. Except sometimes so many people are trying to head so many different directions at once that no one actually goes anywhere at all. Of course, even then, being idiots, people will still push, and the result is that your feet, unable to budge, stay where they are, but your upper body is forced to lean—sideways, backwards, forwards—and if you weren't being held up by the shoulders of those around you, you would topple over. You are completely powerless, and to shove back would only make things worse, and so it is wise at such times to give in to the whims and madness of the big crush, smile apologetically as you are squashed into the people around you, shrug, chuckle, say, "Sorry, sorry." It is, after all, from the right perspective, a comic scene, a couple hundred of us caught in this cornfield shuffle, bending and tilting like wheat in the wind, or like an army of those punchable rubber clowns that always bounce back up. Of course, when you're in the middle of it, it's hard to have any perspective, much less the right one.

While such mass anti-migrations may be the extreme, the norm on the main floor—hot, hectic, harried—is not much better. (It is partly for this reason that the lofty perspective of a roomy VIP area can sometimes be not just a luxury but a necessity, so that you can stand up there with space to breathe and look down at the madness and say to yourself, *Thank God I'm up here.*) But it's not just the claustrophobic conditions that make the whole scene down there so horrendous—it's the unnecessary negativity. People shoving, scowling, barreling through the crowd without a thought: Tall, stunning women with the flush of annoyance on their perfect cheeks push aside littler people like they don't exist, can't possibly be important; big, dumb guys intentionally give you the hard shoulder of their striped shirt as they pass, their narrow eyes hoping for a reaction, for any reason to let their clenched fists fly.

And me, well, negotiating my way through a crowd is one of the few true skills I actually have when it comes to the night. I pause and step aside to let people pass the other direction, which keeps the flow going. I seek out spaces, openings, I swerve and shake and dance my way through them to the beat, sucking in my belly to squeeze through the tight spots. And knowing how it feels to get barreled over, I always have a free hand in front of me, giving people friendly pats on the shoulder to move them gently aside, saying "Excuse me," smiling and saying "Sorry" when I bump someone unintentionally—common courtesies somehow far too uncommon in the night.

Yes, I know what it's like to get knocked aside by some meathead bristling with bravado and muscles who doesn't even have the courtesy to say "Excuse me." It happens tonight, as it does at some point almost every night you go out. There you are, negotiating your way calmly through the madness, dishing out preemptive strikes of kindness as you go, and then some big idiot coming the opposite direction gives you a lowered shoulder full of attitude, spills half your drink on your pants, and doesn't even glance over to apologize.

And you kind of just have to take it. Because if, as is instinct, you shove him back, or throw the remainder of your drink in his face, your evening could be over right there. There is no way to win a fight out at night. Even if you're a martial arts badass and manage to knock the fucker out with a single kung fu strike, you never know how many of his friends are right behind him, ready to jump in. Then there are the bouncers, the highly skilled hulks who, somehow noticing commotion almost before it begins, will be on you in a flash. Yes, get into a brawl at a club and you will inevitably end up being dragged to the door by a bouncer, your head locked in the vise of his tree-trunk arm, and no matter how big or strong or adept at combat you are, attempting to resist these guys is just plain stupid. (Besides, there are more important things to fight out at night than people.)

So you swallow it, you let the guy bump you and walk on by because confrontation is not your style, but all that negative energy passes right into you nonetheless. You feel for a moment something like rage—some dark, angry bird flapping and pecking at the inside of your rib cage—and you take deep breaths to calm it, but it doesn't always work. And I'm an easygoing guy, as good as the next duck at letting stuff slide off my back, but even I get affected by some of the nonsense out here. Then there I am, a generally good-natured pacifist, wanting to punch something, or kick someone in the head. There I am, the last optimist in the New York night, wanting to give up and go home. Yes, even if you do your best not to let that sort of crap get to you, it can color your vision of the night nonetheless, as if someone has slipped sickly yellow contact lenses over your eyes. . . .

Just a simple snap, and things can so quickly turn dark. And it's not just idiots bowling you over who will do it to you, either. There can be any number of instigators: the bartender who seems bent on serving everyone at the bar but you, the guardian of the VIP room who won't let you pass, the girl who responds to your friendly, innocent remark with a toss of cold shoulder and an ugly roll of beautiful eyes. Even something unintentional, someone carelessly singeing your hand with a cigarette, or spilling their cocktail on you, can be the last straw.

And then it doesn't matter how good you were feeling before. Now, wherever you look, everything seems off: all these drunk, desperate bastards, meanness in their laughter and their white teeth flashing vicious, plastic smiles, and the fucking music sucks and you just paid fourteen dollars for a drink you waited fourteen minutes for and now you're wearing seven bucks of it on your pants because of some dickhead. Things are simply not as they should be, and everywhere you look you see not the easy joy of the night, but something else: haughty young women with their self-important postures and cold eyes looking down at everything, guys with chins rigid as cliffs, jaws clenched and biting at something hard, won't let go. . . . So many people who simply won't let go.

And it's ridiculous. I mean, what the hell is wrong with us? Isn't the night supposed to be the place where we can let go of all this crap? And yeah, you could say, "What on earth do *these* people have to worry about?" And the answer is: Who knows? Who knows what it is tonight, what thing you are out here trying not to think of—you tell me: Maybe it's work, maybe it's money, maybe it's an argument you had with a friend, or a girlfriend, or a relative, maybe it's the fact that you have a parent who is ill, or dying, or dead, maybe you have broken up with your love, and there is that sickness in your heart. Maybe it's the fact that you are an adult now, and you're supposed to know what you're doing with this life, but you don't—beneath your grown-up exterior you're still just a scared kid, lost as ever. Yes, maybe it's nothing so specific, maybe it's just the big darkness underneath it all, that unnameable thing that is wrong with life, the thing we all somehow seem to be running from and falling into at once. Maybe it's just everything, the endless exhaustions of being a human being, maybe it's nothing, maybe it's just that you are out here once again, trying your very best to let go and just for once have a good time free of it all, but it's not working. . . . Yes, maybe it's just been a bad day, and the night doesn't seem to be helping.

And sometimes that's almost the worst part. Because this is the place and time meant to wash these burdens away, meant to lighten your load and let you just enjoy for a minute, but the fact is you're not. Your grand hope—that the night will cure you, dissolve your worries like snow into sea—is not always the reality. Actually, the fact that you're out here among all this happy joy and celebration and yet not feeling it frankly just pisses you off more. Yes, being depressed in the night is the worst place to feel that way, it's like having your own personal rain cloud in the midst of a sunny paradise. As during the holidays (and what is the night if not holiday?) your own bad mood gleams, you feel like a pariah for not feeling it, like a pauper on Madison Avenue, all that much worse 'cause everyone else seems to be doing so well.

But though there's supposed to be such a clear division between the day and the night, and your corresponding selves, it's not that simple. It's not like just because it's the night and you have a beer in your hand, all that other shit magically disappears. In fact, hope for this too much, for some final liberation granted by the good-hearted night, and you may find your expectations crushed. I myself tumble into this pitfall far too often: I just put so much faith in the night, as if it will provide some easy, ultimate answer, soothe me like an old man easing into a hot bath, that when it doesn't, it feels like I have been betrayed, like my church has let me down. Yes, sometimes the night, the thing that you were hoping would save you, can be the very thing that ruins you. Sometimes you look around and see all the devastation, all the viciousness and haughtiness and unnecessary drama, all these people so far off, and it only confirms the very hopelessness you were attempting to escape. And it sucks.

And then it seems like no one has quite gotten what they're really looking for—the great letdown of the night, everyone defeated, once again. All these tall, awkward children, so lost and looking and finding nothing. An almost desperate act, the night, all this rabid consumption and desire, all these actions attempting a single, yearned-for point: escape. All these secretly hopeful souls trying to get somewhere better, and going nowhere fast.


## PEOPLE LIKE ZOO

When the whole night turns dark, as it sometimes will, you can either give up and go home, or push through it. I do not like to go home. On one level, I consider each of my nights to be a battle of this sort, a fight to break through not only the darkness around me, but my own shadowed vision.

Of course, I don't mean to suggest that everyone is so easily affected by the negativity out here, so burdened with the heavinesses of life, so neck-deep in self-struggle and search, so yearning for escape. Take Zoo, for instance. Ask him if he has any personal issues and he'll say, "Yeah, man, that's just not really my thing." No, Zoo is a simple man, seemingly unburdened by anything more profound than the practicalities of the moment—whether he can work some free drinks, or if he can hook us a table to chill at. It's almost as if the shadows don't occur to him. "I don't have time to sulk," he explained to me once, a salty look on his face, as if even talking about it disturbed him. "Plus, dude, it's like what do I have to be depressed about? I live a good life, you know. Shit."

Zoo's not a religious cat, as far as I know—I've never heard him mention the word *God* unless it's attached to *damn*—but he knows how blessed a life he leads, and that is enough for him. Unlike me, he's not out here trying to overcome anything or get somewhere he's not—you can see it in his unconcerned brow, smooth and worry-free—he's just where he is, and happy to be there. Yes, when it comes to the night, Zoo's just out here to have a good time—not in any sort of a reactionary way, just a good old time, simple as that—and so are a lot of other people. It may even be that the majority of folks are, in essence, just out here to have some fun. Of course, in essence, so am I.

But it's occurred to me that for Zoo, maybe there simply is no dark side to the night. Or maybe it's that in some sort of instinctual way he knows it's not worth giving any of his attention to. Either way, it seems Zoo lives an existence—easygoing, positive, present, focused on only the good—that I myself yearn for.

Me, I see all the angles, all the awkwardness, all the things I wish I wouldn't see, and it's almost because I wish I didn't that I do. I wish I didn't notice all the meanness, the lostness, the misplaced love; I wish I didn't feel it, the darkness, all around me and within me. I wish I had Zoo's perspective, his easy satisfaction. I wish I could cut off my stupid, questioning, over-thinking head and live how Zoo seems to live—from the gut.

## THE PERFECT ESCAPE?

It shouldn't be such a struggle. The night is not supposed to be a battlefield. I should not be out here wrestling myself as if I contained my own worst enemy. This place is meant for good times and only good times. Laughter, dancing, drinking, celebration. The night and its haunts are designed from their very core to help you ignore all the rest.

Consider how only certain people are allowed entrance. Yes, this is no gloomy tavern, where toward the back you'll see the old whiskered drunk resting his head on the bar, his pockmarked hand holding the half-empty glass of beer; the rail-thin middle-aged woman with stringy hair and missing teeth, swaying and singing to herself by the jukebox. No, at the clubs I frequent, such obviously depressing sights are absent. Indeed, at first glance, there seems nothing that is not perfect. The women are stunning and slender, the men are handsome, well dressed, finely groomed. Even the bathrooms sparkle and gleam and smell nice, the bow-tied man in there to hand you fresh paper towels and mints, your choice of cologne. Yes, these places do a wonderful job of eliminating almost everything you'd rather not see, and anything that does shatter this surface world—the girl who gets too drunk and bails into a set of tables, the aggressive guy who gets in a shouting match with the manager, anyone making any kind of a negative scene whatsoever— these people are ushered out of there so swift and silent you may wonder if they ever even existed. Yes, everything in these places is set just so. On the surface, it's the fucking Garden of Eden. . . .

And these clubs do their damnedest to keep that surface intact. The great volume of music requires conversations to skirt only the most superficial issues. Lights flash and in them you see faces, but you get only the most cursory glance, and with that glance you must make your decision whether or not to attempt to dig deeper. But no one really wants to dig too deep. People almost seem to depend on the shallowness of the night, to take comfort in its most basic sights and sounds: that fine body on the girl who wandered by, the good-hearted bullshitting of friends, this fat, funky beat. It is a good illusion, and we do our best to get lost in it.

This is what these dimly lit shadows promise: a chance to turn away from all the deeper, darker things of life, and you can see it in our horse-blinded eyes, looking straight ahead, pushing forward into the night, trying so hard to block out all the rest. Yes, though all we might do is stand around, our motion seems nonetheless one of perpetual flight, a movement forever away from whatever it is we are trying to escape. And there is always something to turn to: another cigarette, another drink, another doobie, another thing that allows you to shift your focus from whatever dark, empty place it had wandered to onto something simpler, something real right there in your hand. There are a thousand wonderful things to fill those vacant moments, a thousand ways to run away, and so it is that we are never truly still, always going going going, standing up, sitting down, our hands, too, in perpetual motion, banging out bongo beats on the tables and fussing in our pockets for matches and smokes and lighting them up and snatching drinks and swirling ice and taking sips and drags, and our eyes, too, are always shifting, flitting away and back and away again, and our heads are nodding to the beat and our feet are tapping, and the movement never really stops, not really. We won't let it. It's as if we're trying to keep ourselves ceaselessly engaged so that there's not even an instant for anything negative to appear, no way for the darkness to catch us, and with our help, the night almost creates an illusion that stands.

But this sheen of civilization—of pretty faces, laughter, good times—it really is so thin. If it wasn't, why the need for the huge men with the little earpieces watching from the corners? Yes, if there's no darkness, then what exactly is security guarding against? Oh, it teeters on the edge, this polished world. Sometimes it seems like almost anything could topple it over.

Imagine the dreaded nightclub fire, how quickly this celebrating, cultured crowd would become vicious, savage, flames and panic spreading, the slender arms of pretty women cracked and trampled beneath the rush and crush to doors that open inward. Even the heat of words can ignite a place. Something is said or not said, someone else says something back, chests and egos puff up, and it happens— a push, a shove, and then BAM!, fists are flying and friends are jumping in and what began between two drunken fools spreads like some highly contagious disease, rage explodes outward in a perfect circle, and if security doesn't stop it quickly enough, the whole club can descend into madness, bartenders leaping the bar to get involved, bouncers tossing aside tables and couches to get in there and rip people apart and drag them away, grown men breaking bottles on each other's skulls, blood pouring from foreheads, kids in fetal positions on the ground getting kicked, and always one girl sobbing and screaming at the top of her lungs for everyone to *PLEASE STOP!*

But the darkness very rarely breaks through with such violent clarity. More often, it stays hidden, murky, there and yet not there, buried just below the glass of our eyes, and this lovely surface world remains unshattered. But maybe this is the real darkness, the subtle one, hard to get ahold of, hard to name. Because even with all these methods of flight, something dark still remains. You come out here and try to leave life and all its worries behind—and the night does its best to help you—but you cannot, not completely. You dress up in a different costume and put on a different face and drink and drug yourself into a different personality, but all of it at times seems of little use. You are right there.

All of reality is right there, you've only just turned your back on it, and I wonder sometimes if this is as much the problem as the solution. Maybe one of the main reasons for our inability to truly escape is our single-minded attempt to do just that. After all, there's something sinister about this turning away, and there's something dark, too, about the way the night encourages it—concealing all of life's imperfections beneath this thin veil of paradise. It's as if the grand effort at ignoring the dark things, their curious but obvious absence, had resulted in their unmentionable yet unmistakable presence.

And that seems part of the problem: It *is* unmentionable. Beneath this surface existence—the lighthearted bullshitting, the thumping beats, all these faces flashing smiles—there lurks something not quite right, you can sense it, but you're not supposed to discuss it. It's not meant to be mentioned. I am breaking an unwritten rule even bringing this shit up. After all, right now I am addressing the very thing the night seems designed from its core to avoid. Out on the town, people shun anyone who mentions anything too heavy or serious. Tables grow quiet, uncomfortable. But isn't it partly this that makes the darkness so ever-present? Yes, perhaps it's the way everything out here is set just so, none of the darkness allowed, that makes something foul bubble so eagerly just below the surface.

Because this is a dangerous thing to do, smothering all that pain away with the thin lid of the night: It seethes and simmers. Even before it boils over into ego, aggression, chaos, you can feel it there, the nameless instigator of our constant, manic occupations, our quiet, continual self-destruction.

And I'm not saying we should all sit around in the night having heartfelt discussions about our darkest fears, or anything like that. The night should not be group therapy. I just think it's dangerous the way we fly so blindly away, without knowing what we're running from, or where we're going. Maybe this kind of escape was never meant to lead us anywhere good. Maybe all we're really doing is running from darkness into darkness, and we do not even know it.

## DRUGS

Consider the drugs. Ah, the drugs. Without drugs, the night as we know it would not exist. They seem a necessity, alcohol especially. The way a stiff drink will soften your tongue, ease your self-consciousness, smooth you into that social, loose-lipped state of mind. Go out clearheaded, on the other hand, and everything can seem bland, tasteless, boring. Sober, you may feel separate, almost as if everyone else is speaking a foreign language, as if without drugs and alcohol, the night makes no sense. All of which makes me occasionally consider: If you need to be inebriated to enjoy this scene, how fun can it actually be?

There is a very real sense in which the night and all its haunts are nothing more than delivery systems for drugs and alcohol; in other words, maybe we go to these clubs not because of anything intrinsic that they offer, but only because they are places in which we can get all fucked up, and feel at ease doing so. And you do feel at home drinking and smoking away at these spots. In the night, drugs and alcohol are ubiquitous, wonderfully accepted. At this hour, you can get away with doing things—inhaling mass amounts of tobacco and ganja, slurping up enough alcohol to kill a horse, snorting powders that can easily snuff a heart—that were someone to see you doing in the light of day, they'd have no choice but to think: *rehab.* Here in the darkness, it's all so out in the open and almost everyone is participating in one way or another that there's comfort for you and your addictions, plenty of shadows to hide in. (Besides, people will try not to look at you too closely if they do not like what they see. . . . )

It's a good thing, too, that the night allows us our rituals of smoke and liquid and powder. We seem to have a deep social need to imbibe these substances. The idea, the routine, the very occupation calls to us—that ancient urge to have something in your hand to turn to. And in a social situation, it truly is a great comfort to be able to pause from your conversation and take a smooth drag of your smoke, exhale through the corner of your mouth, or to take a casual sip of the cold drink in your hand, swirl it and hear the ice tinkle. Conversely, if it is just you out there with no defense shield—no smoke to clutch between scissored fingers, nor cocktail to swirl and sip on—it can be scary. Without those barriers of smoke and drink to hide behind, it is, after all, just you, naked and vulnerable and awkward, and it is a rare man indeed out at night, and in the world, and a rare woman, too, who can sit and be themselves with nothing in their hands, and want nothing.

Of course, it's not just the rituals of drugging we desire: We want the effects, too. Yes, there is a state of mind—anyone who's had two or three drinks has been there—in which, for a moment or two at least, everything finally just feels right. Your insides are warm, you have a grin on your face involuntarily, you are feeling good, so good you're almost glowing, and everything around you seems to be glowing, too. Humming. After all, the effects of a couple beers and shots (or a toke of a spliff, a bump of *yayo*, a hit of E—pick your poison)—it changes your perspective. It puts you in a place of selective vision. Nothing is so bad anymore, nothing so cruel. The world is a different place when you are drunk, or high, or both. Warmer. Everything seems spectacularly tilted, golden and fuzzy, a leap aside from regular. You've awakened in an alternate universe, and all your concerns and inhibitions seem someone else's now. You have escaped yourself, arrived somewhere else, somewhere better. And this is part of the allure of drugs. They promise to take you somewhere new.

This promised destination need not be one of murky oblivion, either; unlikely as it may seem, drugs can at times lead you to a kind of clarity. Yes, a truly fine buzz can put you in a state of heightened awareness. Sure, you may not remember these moments so perfectly the next day, but right now you are on top of everything, you are lighting people's cigarettes before they even pat their pockets for a match, you are finishing people's sentences when they lose their train of thought, you are stepping out of the way of beautiful waitresses burdened with trays of bottles before they even have the chance to say "Excuse me," you are figuring out the grandest mysteries of life with good friends, your hands are flashing out to steady stumbling strangers, witticisms are flowing from your mouth into the perfect ears of pretty ladies, your eyes are wide open and seeing everything. You are, in a word, unstoppable.

Oh, drugs can be wonderful things, they really can. The pure, simple pleasure of having a shot or a beer with your friends, or of lighting up a smoke, or a doobie—the warmth of liquor spreading through your belly, the thick, heavy feel of smoke in your lungs, the sensation of gripping something solid in your hand, the resulting tilts of consciousness. The simple way these substances can make you feel good. Indeed, what they can help accomplish is an amazing feat, especially amongst all these clenched-up, stressed-out New Yorkers. You can see people relax, open up, smile, shrug all that weight from their shoulders. Suddenly they are themselves again. And this is part of why drugs are so dangerous—they really do seem like such a good answer, in the beginning.

The problem is that this perfect buzz is rarely enough. Even when I've never felt better, still I want more. . . . Still I say yes to another smoke, another spliff, another shot. I mean, by this point in the night, I'm probably pushing twelve drinks, four doobies, a pack or more of smokes: Do I actually want to get more drunk, more high, smoke another goddamn butt? If I took a good look at myself, probably not. (Of course, these drugs are aids in making sure you don't take a good look—like some sort of virus, they seem to perpetuate themselves through spreading blindness and idiocy.) Yes, the wise thing at this point would be to take it easy, enjoy where you are and how you're doing, not push it any further. The problem is, you're not wise—you're drunk—and the last thought in your mind is how another drink will shove you over the edge. After all, you're unstoppable: What's one more shot? Besides, the idea of more, of somewhere even better to go, even if you're already feeling fine—it's an endlessly alluring one. . . .

This is where the whole drug and alcohol thing can go awry. The entire night becomes focused on the next drink, the next bump. Inebriation becomes a sport, a crescendo of consumption. One shot—or even three—is not enough. It is the one after that, and the one after that, that will get us to that point, even if the truth is we're already there. Yes, even if we're already there and couldn't feel any better, it often feels like we continue to chase something down nonetheless, as if there's somewhere we're trying to get, and the drugs and alcohol are the road. The thing is, it is far too easy to take this road too far. . . .

The perfect buzz is a fine, fine line. One shot too many is exactly that—one too many. The room begins to spin in slow, repeating quarter-revolutions. Your awareness—not long ago so heightened—begins to shrink, and quick. Instead of steadying stumbling strangers, you begin to weave and sway yourself, bump into tables, topple drinks. Instead of lighting other people's smokes, cool as Cary Grant, now you are lighting the wrong end of your own, inhaling that plastic filter smoke, coughing your innards out like you have the black lung. You cannot seem to do anything right anymore, not even the things that you've been doing since you were two. You cannot walk without rubber in your legs, you cannot talk without a slur in your voice, you cannot even take a sip of your drink without misjudging the distance between the glass and your mouth and bringing it with a sharp clink to your teeth.

It is not long after the comedy that the tragedy sets in. It usually arrives with a single thought: *I'm not feeling too good.* No longer connected to everyone around you, suddenly you are separate, sitting alone in some forlorn corner with your head in your hands, hiccupping and trying your damnedest to make the room stop lurching, dreading the looming thought that you might feel better if you threw up.

The casualties are everywhere, especially at this hour. I see grown men with both their arms slung over friends' shoulders as if being carried wounded from a battlefield. I see girls who have consumed so much they have simply fallen asleep. I see ghost-white faces specked with cold sweat, so pale you can almost see through them. I see beautiful women beautiful no longer, their faces ruddy and aged prematurely by too many nights of drinking and smoking, their eyes a hazy, sloppy slush, their eyelashes fluttering shut involuntarily, their fine feminine fingers clenching a lonely glass of red wine like it's all they have left. I see good friends whispering and glancing nervously off toward the bathroom in anticipation of their next urgent trip there, their eyes big and sick and eager, their hands wringing, expectant, the little bag of powder in their pocket. I see their eyes returning from the bathroom bigger and sicker and more eager, as if they had been filled with helium, hardly anyone there anymore behind the want.

I see so much ruin out at night. So much darkness in this blind attempt to escape it. So many promising souls destroying themselves. And I know that I am one of them.

After all, taking an honest look at all these fucked-up people is like taking an honest look at one's self, and it's not too pretty a sight. Because I know there are times that I must look much the same, my eyes all hollow and bleary and bloodshot, sweating and swaying and spilling the drink in my hand, slurring scotch-and-ash-scented nonsense to some half-beautiful girl who just turns and walks away. Yes, there have been many times when if I could actually see myself, I would not like what I saw. (Of course, as I mentioned, drugs are excellent at making sure you don't take too good a look. Drugs can be things you turn away to and from, all in the very same moment—the motion of an addict if ever there was one. After all, as you reach for another shot, another joint, another cigarette, you are, at least on one level, seeking to snuff the part of you that asks, *What the fuck am I doing putting these poisons in my body?* Drugs seem to blanket all things, even awareness of themselves. Which is why they're so good at helping you escape, at least for a while. . . . )

But even with the forgetful blanket of inebriation draped across our shoulders, we can no longer plead true ignorance, not really, not anymore. After all, the simple truth is that we are out here imbibing substances that can kill us, that *are* killing us. And this isn't the sixties or seventies anymore, when no one really knew how bad any of it was, when people chain-smoked cigarettes like they were going out of style and blew huge rails of cocaine and had copious amounts of unprotected sex with whomever they wished, and all of it without a single guilty thought. Yes, back then the night was an innocent thing, its citizens enviably oblivious. Now we have AIDS and we know too well what drugs and alcohol can do to us and even the tobacco companies admit that their shit kills. Now we are out here doing this stuff *consciously*. Of course, being young and out at night—your first true evenings hitting the town, just out of college, life all ahead of you and things like death impossible—is probably not so different from living in the seventies. In the young there's still that innocence, that blissfully ignorant thought: *It could never happen to me.* But we aren't living in the seventies, and I'm no longer twenty-two. We're in a new age, and I am getting to the age in my life—nearing thirty—when I am beginning to lose my illusions of all that. I no longer feel the brash immortality of youth. I no longer believe it could never happen to me. (It is happening to me: My throat and lungs are scarred from all that smoke, and the alcohol and pot has left the blade of my mind less than sharp. Sure, I may not be snorting fat rails of cocaine off hookers' asses every night or sticking a needle in my vein, but I'm out here killing myself nonetheless. *And I know it.*)

And it sucks that we have to live in an age of such consciousness, a time when we can't even do something as simple as smoke a cigarette without knowing what a completely stupid and dangerous choice it is we're making. But it's not just our awareness of it that makes the whole situation so shitty: On an even more basic level, what really sucks is the plain, long-lamented fact that all this stuff that can be so much fun, so liberating, has to be so bad for you. . . . That so many of our methods for celebration, for in a sense, *living,* have to be so closely tied to death. It kills me that it all has to be so wrapped up in self-destruction, so teetering on the edge of madness. That such an innocent, human desire—to get to somewhere better—can lead right back around to such darkness, one way or the next.

And sure, there might be something enticing about flirting with disaster, dancing on the edge of destruction—akin to the sickeningly wonderful feeling of having unprotected sex with someone you just met—but I don't want to die, I really don't. The problem is, I don't want to lose this life of the night, either. And that's what scares me—that to be a healthy person, I'll have to give up the night, all its endless wonders and possibilities. I am caught in an awful circle—this world I love is killing me. Or maybe it is simply me that is killing me, the night only a cold, dark observer. Either way, it sometimes seems the only way for me to survive might be to let go of the thing I love the most. . . .

I guess love affairs with the night rarely last long. I've known guys who have OD'd, guys who have died. I've had close friends—good kids without a harmful bone in their bodies—who somehow took this scene too far and ended up in rehab. As a result, they've had no choice but to completely cut the night out of their lives for the sake of their health and sanity. Except for perhaps a birthday dinner, or a game of cards, they will hardly even emerge after dark.

## SEEING THROUGH THE DARK

Love affairs with the night don't always end in such clear disaster, with rehab and overdoses and death. As with any normal relationship, so it can be with the night: Sometimes you just get sick of the bitch. . . .

This is the real reason a lot of my good friends have left this scene behind. It's as if they decided they just no longer had the patience for it. Take Stibbs, who, with his easily amused demeanor and propensity for couches, is about as laid-back a guy as you will encounter, and sure, he's here tonight, sipping on his twelve-year-old scotch and giggling like a kid who's not much older, but for the most part, his nightlife is a thing of the past. "There's just so much fucking bullshit at these places," I remember him saying one night a few years back, after he'd just been bumped by some meathead, "and I just don't have the will to wade through it anymore." He was angry, and there is nothing more unnerving than seeing a really friendly guy get angry. "I mean, why would I want to bother?" he hissed. Or take what Hobbes said awhile back, with less wryness than usual in his grin—"I went out Tuesday, Wednesday, and Thursday, and what do I have to show for it?"

Why *would* I want to bother? What *do* I have to show for it? Yes, these are good questions, and recently I've been finding myself asking them more and more often, and others, too. Like, what am I really doing out here, and where exactly is this night leading us all anyway?

Sometimes you just get to the point where you feel the need to take stock of things. And when you look around at the reality of the situation, it can seem pretty ugly. All these people out here for their own good and no one else's. "It's so selfish," someone once reminded me. "It's like eating." And maybe it's no good for the self, either. Maybe the night is just some sweet call of the sirens, lulling us into false beliefs and a kind of sleep. All of us wrapped up in one wrong answer or the next. Everyone off. Everyone out here so blindly fleeing from darkness into further darkness. No true light out here in the night, only this big bright illusion, and behind it, beneath it, nothing.

And then no matter how hard you try to come up with hopeful, positive answers to those questions, you just can't: *Why bother?* I don't know. *What to show for it?* Nothing. *What am I doing here?* I don't know. *Where is it leading me?* No-where.

Yes, look where the night has led me in the long run. Nowhere, really. I mean, here I am, nearing thirty, and I'm still basically doing the same crap I was ten years ago. And that's the kind of magical (and sinister) thing about the night: It freezes time, and you along with it. This lifestyle encourages little growth. No, going out night after night and getting your shit together don't really mix. It's just too hard to wake up the next day and begin again, start fresh, do the things you know you should do. You're too hung over. You say to yourself, *Tomorrow,* which after the next night will mean the day after tomorrow, and so on—whole months, years, lifetimes blending into one long bleary day and indeterminate night.

Yes, after all these years, here I still am, out here avoid-ing real life and clinging to my youth, a big scared kid in grown-ups' clothes. And just what the hell is this costume I'm wearing, anyway? This jacket and tie thrown on in an odd attempt at irony, my purposely disheveled hair and nine-day beard, the old army watch from the sixties on my wrist, my scuffed black boots, this American Spirit ciga-rette in my hand even though my mom is sick with em-physema. Just who the fuck do I think I am? Oh, I may put up a good front, but underneath there are times I literally tremble.

And what the hell is this look on my face right now, this wolf mask of despair? Yes, look where the night has led me tonight! Shit, this is the second time this evening I've found myself all glum and brooding and wishing for some-thing else. Standing here with this mass of negativity rushing through my chest, ready to pummel the next guy who looks at me wrong, and why?—all because some jerk with attitude bumped me, and half of my drink spilled on my pant leg, making it look like I'd peed myself.

What am I, a little girl? Well, yes, I guess so, 'cause right now I feel like one, like some angry, dejected lover of the night, stood up and let down once again. And nothing around me really seems to be helping at the moment, either, all this flight and self-destruction, all these faces slashed with sneers and practiced disgust, and the DJ's playing some bad eighties butt-rock tune for some reason, and I don't even want to dance anymore, not really, I don't want to do anything, I just want to stand here and brood, and so that is what I do. I stand exactly where I am, my fists and shoulders clenched and my jaw, too, the stain on my pants now wet against my skin, and like some stubborn boulder, I refuse to budge. I just stand here smoldering and make everyone go around me, which they do cautiously, as they can see the rage rippling off me like heat off a hot black road.

Is this wretched beast really me? Is this miserable muppet what I've become? Except it's not just me. A lot of other people out here have similar expressions on their faces. And it's ridiculous, all these miserable people. A comic tragedy how serious we have become. What the fuck could possibly actually be wrong? I mean, here I am, in a place that's meant solely for having a good time, and I'm moping? About what, some fuckhead that bumped me?

And so sometimes, when I notice the darkness of the night, and of myself, I cannot help but shake my head and grin at it all—at me and my absurd dismay, at all the outlandishly disappointed faces we put on in the night, at all the absurd circumstances, at everyone, myself especially, just so far off.

Yes, it is good at such times, before your mood descends into further gloom, to take a step back and recognize that none of this shit matters even a little. Who cares that some guy bumped you and didn't apologize? (Know that the guy is fighting harder battles than you could engage him in.) Who cares if the bartender's taking everyone else's orders but not your own, or if the VIP-room bouncer won't let you in? (Know that their nights have been a hell of a lot worse than yours.) Who cares about any of that crap? If there is anything wrong with this picture, it is not the night itself—after all, the night is the way it is, filled with all sorts of nonsense—but you, you for fooling yourself into thinking any of it matters.

And that's the kind of strangely wonderful thing about all the nonsense out here. Because when you finally see how completely fucked and worthless so much of this night is, then you can look at what's left. Then you can look at the things that matter. And there are very few things that really do matter out at night: your friends, the possibility of love, and the sweet effort of celebration.

Yes, you might not think it, but this attempt to come out here and celebrate, it is important, in the end. Because as much as it can be ugly, it can be beautiful, too. Though this urge to escape might lead us to some pretty dark places, the motive, to be happy, free, to live, if only for a little, well, shit, man—that's what it's all about. We're all just out here trying to get to somewhere better. Who cares if we have lost our way? So has everyone else in the universe. The fact that we are trying to get there, our tireless effort, is at least a beginning.

Because it would be so easy not to do this, to give up on life and the night, to give into despair. There is plenty of evidence to support such a choice. And this is why the night really is a beautiful decision, in the end. Because it makes no sense. Indeed, it seems almost incomprehensible that out of all this, out of this great heavy existence of life, here we are anyway, in spite of and because of it all, dancing our way through the dark. I mean, what an odd thing. What with all that happens in this heartbreaking world, all the ugliness that life and the night dish out, what a strange occurrence. How could we celebrate after all this?

How could we not?

Yes, when faced with the grand beautiful ugly all of this night, and of this life, it's really the only thing left to do. Because when you look at it all clearly, there's no time not to celebrate. Life is very short, and so are these nights. There is really only just enough time for one more dance.

## 6

## Dancing: A Self-Conscious White Man's Guide

> Those who were dancing were thought to be insane by those who couldn't hear the music.
>
> —FRIEDRICH NIETZSCHE

**WHEN I GO OUT,** I need to dance. It's like some sort of strange moral imperative. If I don't get my groove on, then I just can't consider it a successful evening out.

Fortunately, my only real requirement for any night—that, if only for a minute or two, I shake my butt to some funky music—is a theoretically easy one to fulfill. Yes, in a night filled with far-fetched possibilities and expensive dreams—beautiful women you will not meet and VIP rooms you will not get into—dancing is one of the few certainties. When you are out at night and there is music, you can always dance. It is the only action that requires nothing of anyone but you. Though it might help, you need not be inebriated to do it. These days, you do not even need a partner. And unlike everything else out at night, dancing is free.

Of course, it's never as simple as it sounds. For one thing, the dance floor is perpetually jam-packed, cramped and breathless, and it always seems like there are more people standing around it or pushing through it than actually dancing on it. And the ones who are dancing tend to do it with a necessary kind of aggression, fighting for position and maintaining their hard-won perimeters with sharp elbows and angry looks, so that heading out there willingly can seem a rather odd choice. But it's not just the physical inconveniences of trying to dance in a place like this that make it tough—it's the mental ones, too.

Because there's something kind of awkward about dancing, if you're not in exactly the right frame of mind for it. I mean, just what the fuck are we doing out there, anyway? What an absurd activity, all those people wiggling around to loud noises. It seems some semi-voluntary form of epilepsy, some disease. People look afflicted.

Yes, consider how outlandish the whole act would look were you to remove the music. I actually experienced this recently, over at this crazy festival in Denmark called Roskilde—five different stages, everyone from Snoop Dogg to Duran Duran performing live, seventy thousand alternative Europeans dancing their hearts out—and out of all the madness, the beautiful Nordic women and the giant hash spliffs and the massive rave tent where the music bumped till the northern sun came out at four in the morning, the most absurd thing I saw the whole weekend was what lay within this huge golf ball–like structure that sat in the dust of the food court. Inside, two hundred people wearing big silver earphones were twisting and turning and jumping around a dance floor in a marked and utter quiet. And until you, too, put on the headphones, there was no music, only the sound of shoes shuffling on the floor, and I can't tell you how weird it looked, a bunch of people moving their bodies to silence. You felt immediately like you had entered some alternate universe whose sounds you could not hear; you felt like you were tripping on acid. You would have thought they were some strange cult of madmen, the way they writhed around ecstatically to a voice only they could hear, or maybe you'd think you had stumbled upon some field of drunken, disoriented soldiers, marching haphazardly in wobbly, senseless circles, bumping into each other and grinning idiotically, waving their hands in the air as if signaling some indiscriminate general on a distant hilltop. (Of course, all you had to do was put on the headphones, which smiling festival workers handed to you as you entered, and you became one of the people on the inside of this strange cult, the music flooded your ears and you started dancing yourself, and it no longer seemed so weird.) Yes, but view the act of dancing from some sort of objective perspective—take a look at the dance floor of a club from behind soundproof glass, for instance—and it becomes an ultimately absurd act, comic and ridiculous-looking to no end.

Shit, even with music, the whole thing looks ridiculous. All around me tonight, out here on the dance floor of this "civilized" club, people are pulling the most outlandish maneuvers: Some hop and twist and step like chickens, some do the jitterbug, the shopping cart, the sprinkler, the lasso, some raise the roof, some suppress the floor, some shift from foot to foot like uncomfortable pigeons, or writhe like orgiastic snakes, some stand motionless with their arms crossed and imperceptibly nod their heads to the beat, some dance close, limbs all intertwined, and basically dry-hump each other right there in front of everyone.

And it's not just what we do with our bodies: Our faces pull some strange shit, too. Yes, the expressions we make when we dance are almost as funny as the ones we make while having sex. You know, the lips sucked in like you're holding in your last breath, or pursed out like Mick Jagger's—or a gorilla giving birth—or the eyes scrunched shut like if they weren't, your soul might jump right out of them, or like the music touched you so deeply it hurt. Yes, there is the "it feels so good it hurts" look, forehead appropriately pained, that badass scowl of pleasure accompanied by the rock-star hair-toss head-bop, maybe an index finger tossed in the air and thrust to the beat to emphasize the point that someone or something around here is number one. Ugly faces, stupid faces, beautiful faces. There are expressions of concentrated boredom, glazed eyes looking off into the distance, there are blissed-out expressions of true serenity, huge grins spread across faces washed clean and finally just happy.

And when you're aware of how everyone else looks ridiculous, it's hard not to be aware that you look ridiculous, too. I'm a complete idiot on the dance floor, and I know this. I mean, when I really get into it, there I am, sticking out my butt and rotating it to the beat, or swinging my arms like an orangutan, or shaking my mane around like a lion on LSD, or jumping up and down like a dog trying to get a biscuit that's just out of reach, and making all sorts of appropriately stupid-ass faces to match, no doubt.

Now, on a very basic level, this seems to counteract many of one's previous motives of the night. All your concerted efforts to look suave—the way you dressed up or down, the too-cool-for-school scowl you painted so consciously on your face, all those ways you tried so hard to appear a certain way, badass, above it all, icily removed—all of that is eliminated and utterly undermined the moment you step out onto the dance floor and do your particular version of the Macarena, or shake your booty to some ABBA song. Yes, it's strange, but people really do tend to undo themselves out there. Consider the pretty little white girls who probably went to Sarah Lawrence and majored in Women's Studies singing along to all the lyrics of completely misogynistic songs about bitches and hoes, their little asses shaking, all sense of injustice, for the moment, forgotten; consider pacifists like me throwing a pistol-shaped hand in the air and thrusting it to the *rat tat tat* of machine-gun gangsta bass. Yes, it doesn't matter who you are: If you get out there and shake your thing, you run a high risk of completely discrediting yourself and everything you stand for. After all, how can anyone—including you—take you seriously when you're gyrating around like a crippled hooker on crack?

## THE BATHROBE BOOGIE

I probably shouldn't admit it, but some of my happiest moments as a human being on this earth have been dancing around alone in my apartment. Just out of the shower, the music blasting—old-school Jamaican ska and weird Latino mambo beats you'd never really hear at the clubs I frequent—and I am busting crazy salsa moves I would never dare attempt on a real dance floor, my hips are shifting and my feet are stepping and I am spinning and jumping up and down and skipping across the wooden floor and spreading my arms like wings and my wet hair and bathrobe's tails are whirling and there is this giant grin on my face and not a single thought in my head and the music is throwing my body all around the room and I am letting it. And I am a happy man. Yes, for no particular reason that I can think of, except for some basic joy that I won't let poke its head out very often, I am dancing.

The thing is, I know no one can see me, and even though I know it shouldn't, this somehow makes all the difference in the world. It is a strange thing, but it seems we are a species that dances most freely in the invisible solitude of our apartments, that sings most lovely in the shower.

When I'm out on the dance floor of a nightclub, potentially watched by a thousand eyes (or just the two belonging to a beautiful creature across from me), it's an entirely different situation. Yes, toss a partner into the mix, a pretty woman, for instance, and I go to pieces. Part of it is the simple fact that I just don't dance very well with a partner—her hips always seem to go one direction, mine the other, I try to spin her one way, she goes the opposite, and my nose bonks into her eyebrow, and there is much apologizing and embarrassed grinning and avoiding of eyes and a great struggle within myself to just relax and dance as if there was no one in front of me, which is a ridiculous thing to do: I mean, why dance with someone if all you're focused on is pretending they're not there? But even if I'm not stepping on her toes, there's something about the grand mating-ritual act of it, the fact that *I AM DANCING WITH A MEMBER OF THE OPPOSITE SEX,* that always gets me. Because when you're out there with someone you just met, it's supposed to be this very serious moment—the first dance, full of important maneuvers and subtle symbols. But me, I don't know, I can never seem to keep a straight face. I try my best to dance with her as I should, keeping my countenance very cheek-boned and serious and sexy, rotating my hips in a certain way, but I cannot. The whole thing is utterly absurd, and it is all I can do to keep from bursting out laughing. As it is, I have a huge, stupid grin on my face that I'm trying to suppress, and the girl must think I'm crazy.

But I can't blame my poor partner for all the awkwardness and neuroses I feel on the dance floor. Even when I'm out there on my own, dancing solo, I still feel a kind of constraint. I want to let go and dance freely—in fact, there's nothing in the world I want more—but cannot, not really. I am too aware of how I must look, the foolishness of my movements, the ridiculousness of the act, and the results are tangible. I dance stiff, timid, duck-footed. My shoes feel stuck to the floor, my hips feel frozen, my eyes glance around nervously, wondering who might be watching.

And I'm not the only one. I see this side to a lot of people out at night—fearful, all clenched up, unable to let themselves go. Yes, even here, in this city that prides itself on its wildness, people are remarkably reserved. Afraid to let loose, afraid to even dance. And even if they do get up the courage to dance, the majority, like me, proceed cautiously, awkwardly, too aware of themselves through other people's eyes.

The thing is, though the night seems geared in so many ways to help you find a sense of freedom—the alcohol to ease your inhibitions, the darkness to shroud you in anonymity—there are other aspects of the night that work against such liberation. The way everyone's so viciously voyeuristic, so ready with narrow eyes to pounce on anything out of the ordinary and judge it. It's not all paranoia, either: People really are people-watching, and so if you get out there and let yourself go, you are indeed opening yourself up to ridicule. Cute girls perch on the edge of the dance floor, giggling and pointing: "I'm sorry to interrupt," I once asked two girls who were in the middle of this, "I was just wondering: What are you guys doing?" "We're looking at all the people trying too hard," the brunette explained. "It's really fun," furthered the blonde. Or I think back to a Halloween party I had, sitting in a lion costume on my battered couch next to this slender, stunning, brown-haired model, and she turns to me and points at one of my good college friends, Spanish Ben, who is out there dancing himself free and funky, his head down doing the fast jog-in-place boogie, and says, "God, *he* must be drunk."

It's a strange tug and pull, losing yourself in the night. It's like you're encouraged to get your freak on—that seems one of the night's most basic goals—but only up to a point, only just so much, and only in the established ways, or people will start to look at you weird. No one wants the boat too rocking, that glassy surface of the lake disturbed. No one wants to see beneath the skin—a human being's true face seems too bright, too beautiful strange for such dark places—and no one wants anything that makes them feel uncomfortable, or shatters the status quo. And there's something almost Orwellian about it, the way, even more than the bouncers lurking in dark corners, or the hidden cameras in the ceilings, it is our very own peers, watching and judging us with their sneers and vicious whispers, who keep us in line.

And even more than them, it's us. It's so out there in this society night—this grand concern with appearance, with what is proper, accepted, normal—it's somehow ended up in here. It is a system of control that finds its final confirmation—or denial—in our very own minds. We police ourselves. I am my own restraining order, always second-guessing myself, always afraid of doing something stupid, always petrified of being mocked, always holding myself back from putting myself out there, restricting myself from letting go.

I don't know what my problem is. All I can say for sure is that there really are times that I feel caged by the presence of other people's eyes. As if nearly everything I do is permeated, almost on a subconscious level, by a deep-seated need to have people look at me in the right way—or rather, *not* look at me in the *wrong* way. Because it's not so much that I necessarily want praise in their eyes, I just don't want condemnation, I just don't want to be mocked. Yes, though I know in some theoretical sense that I shouldn't give a flying fuck what a bunch of strangers think about me, I do. Though my mind wishes it were beyond such ridiculous concerns, my body feels them nonetheless—the response is a physical, visceral one. Sometimes I literally tremble like one of those pathetic little hairless dogs. My body, my blood, my very atoms scream for me to act suave, calm, collected, shut off from all potential ridicule, socially accepted to the point of near invisibility. And on one level it makes sense. You kind of have to care what you look like, since at some base core of you, that is why you're out here, to spread and strut your peacock feathers. You're on display, especially when you're dancing, shaking it and letting the other sex know what you got. In this way, the whole self-consciousness thing may actually stem from a kind of biological imperative—your instincts telling you not to look too stupid or you might not get laid and spread your genes. After all, who wants their child to dance like an idiot?

And it's a shame. I mean, what's the night good for if not as a place to get beyond all that crap, a place to get a little weird? Now, I'm not advocating biting chicken's heads off or rocking out with your cock out or breaking bottles over people's skulls or anything necessarily violent or criminal, I'm just talking about getting a little funky on the dance floor, fucking shit up a bit, having a little fun. . . . But for me, and for many others, it's not so easy. Yes, even here, where it's supposed to be all about freedom, we feel too acutely the invisible chains of propriety, and of our own self-awareness. Even here, people hang on to themselves so tightly, and they will not let go. Many of us will not even dance.

## EXHIBITIONISTS, AND OTHERS WITH ALL OR NO EGO

Of course, not everyone is like this. There seem to be others the disease of self-consciousness does not afflict. Instead, they seem to bask in the voyeurism of the night, feed off the knowledge that other people's eyes are on them. Yes, they're out there on the dance floor knowing they are being watched and loving every minute of it. Just earlier tonight, for instance, G and I found ourselves perched on the edge of the madness, checking out this girl who was out there dancing with herself. She was a stunning thing and knew it: the long blond hair, the little black miniskirt, the big unnecessary sunglasses on that perfect face, every writhing movement of her little body saturated in sex.

"Look how fucking *sexy* she dances," G said.

"That's why she's out there," I replied, " 'cause she knows she looks good. It's like a self-perpetuating ego trip."

"Exactly! It's like she's fucking herself on the dance floor!"

The self-assured, narcissistic way she moved. Chewing bubble gum, even. And she knew G and I and every other guy who could see her was watching her, and this seemed to feed her movements, fill and expand them, as if she was just soaking it all up.

You'll see this every now and then out at night, almost like people are putting on shows, performances. Take the two young models grinding it out together on the dance floor, looking hot and knowing it. They can't be over twenty, one in a one-piece white minidress, her darker features and brown hair and tight fine body, the ass and small tits, the other a pure blonde, classic America, in a red-flower dress that's also short and poofs out at the hips, so that you see skin and thigh on both of these creatures, these stunning young things, and it's just not right what they're doing out there, it's not fair—their hands all over each other, their fine golden legs intertwined and rubbing and pushing up tiny skirts, and Jesus Christ, there is no finer sight in the night than two beautiful women simulating sex out on the dance floor, it is enough to make any normal man a vicious voyeur, it is enough to make us slip on puddles of our own drool, it is enough, no, it is too much, *Jesus Christ,* you think, *how the fuck do they do that?*—their slender hips almost dislocated from the rest of their body, pressed up against each other, snapping in fine rhythmic circles to the beat, connected at the waist but their two torsos leaning way back, their breasts taut and the nipples perking out. . . . And then they even dare to kiss—they bring their torsos back in so that their breasts mash against each other and draw their heads in close and give each other their wet tongues—and it is too much, and they know it, they know they are driving us crazy, and they love it. And sure, they are enjoying themselves just dancing and doing their thing, but they seem to be enjoying even more the astonished eyes of everyone watching them, they are bathing in a sea of gazes, orgasmic as much from the exhibition as from the act itself. The performance swells. I force my eyes away out of awe and shame.

Then there's another breed of dancer. They're not exactly exhibitionists—they're not out there to be seen, per se—but they don't mind being looked at, either. Fatdog is like this. So is Whitey. I don't know if it's all ego or none, but it's one of the two. All that's certain is they are confident enough to put themselves out there without a second thought: So it is that you will see Fatdog grab some random hot little thing he's never even met and just start rocking the forbidden dance with her, or lifting her up and tossing her about like an orca with a seal in its teeth, literally flipping her over his shoulder and swinging her around and pulling all sorts of ridiculous old-school jitterbug moves. Yes, out on the dance floor, Fatty is all action and no mind, no second-guessing, this huge, mischievous, puppy-dog grin spread all over his face. And he's so himself, such an innocently forthright monster, that there's just no stopping him, and even girls who would reject ninety-nine percent of the guys who ask them to dance will let the Dog swing them around for a little bit, if only out of a kind of pitying curiosity toward the oddly confident mutt before them. (Of course, it hardly matters if there's no girl to accompany him—Fatdog has no qualms getting out there on his own and busting his limited but nonetheless impressive repertoire of break-dance maneuvers without a speck of self-consciousness.)

Then there is Whitey, who is one of my favorite people in the world to watch dance. True to his nickname, he's as white as you get—the straight blond hair parted just so, the memberships at all the right golf and tennis and beach clubs in the Hamptons, his job on Wall Street—but the guy's got soul nonetheless. Not that he's necessarily a suave dancer. In fact, he looks pretty silly—his torso leans way forward and a little to the side; his butt sticks way out behind and rotates to the beat; his head tilts as if he's questioning something he's confused about; his arms spread out to the sides for balance. And then, in this rather awkward position, leaning forward with wings half extended, his whole body kind of bobs up and down like an excited parrot. But on his face is just the most blissful smile, it washes his features clean and smooth and his eyes are closed like heaven's right there on the inside of his eyelids, and he just doesn't give a damn how ridiculous he looks—he's having too much fun.

And somehow this is a little different, a little more beautiful than someone out there putting on a show, even if it is a show as overwhelmingly enticing as the lesbian mash. There's something about someone dancing simply because they want to and for no baser reasons, someone who can really just let themselves go, fling their arms and hair around, jump up and down, foolish and happy and free. I love people who don't give a fuck, who can just do their thing and have a good time doing it. It's so rare, so refreshing, so inspiring.

Yes, there are inspirations out here, shining things in the darkness who somehow get what the night—what life—is really all about. Just looking at them can make you feel better. Like the cute little brunette in a white skirt bouncing around with this giant sweetness all over her. You see her dancing with this big smile and good vibes just emanating and when she comes near you, hops your direction, she catches you looking at her, dumbstruck, your eyes as wide as moons. And then she smiles at you, and you can barely look at her anymore, she's so packed full of sunshine and beautiful bright, and so maybe you swallow hard and look down and away, but maybe you don't, maybe when she smiles at you, you smile back and say to yourself, *Fuck it*, and now you are dancing, too, shaking all that weight and worry from your shoulders because this beautiful thing has reminded you to.

Oh, man, and all I want to do in the end is dance, just dance, but as much as I wish I had the ego of the exhibitionist, the lack of self-consciousness of Fatty or Whitey, the courage and freedom of this sun-eyed girl, I do not. Such a state of pure existence on the dance floor is no easy thing to attain, especially if you're a somewhat shy, socially anxious cat like me. Yes, getting to a point of liberation out there has always been a battle. But sometimes you just have to hook it.

## DANCING FOOL

Oh, it's tough for me out there. Even when drunk and stoned—and by this time, I most surely am—I'm still just too goddamn aware: of myself, of the eyes around me, of the whole mating-ritual, chicken-strutting, peacock-feather-spreading act of dancing, and so there will be that moment or minute or five when I first get out there on the dance floor—and periodic relapses thereafter—when I feel naked, on camera, justifiably awkward, and my hips are tight and my knees have a touch of tremble when they bend to the beat.

Every night I attempt to dance, I find myself in this situation, with this wall of self-consciousness to break through. And it's hard to say exactly how I do it—what it is, finally, that allows me to overcome my fear and dance. It seems a mystical decision, almost an act of faith, like stepping off a ledge into mist. You kind of just have to say, "Fuck it," and throw yourself out there.

Or perhaps it is not so much "fuck *it*" as it is "fuck *you*"—not a "fuck you" to any one person or thing, but to everyone and everything, to the part of you and of everyone and of life that is keeping you chained, that is holding you back from really living and loving and dancing the way you know you could. And so you just kind of rebel against the drab formality of yourself and of your life as it usually is, you rebel against the fear in yourself and all the other shit that's not worth a damn, and though there are all these things holding you back from dancing, you do it anyway, you get out there and shake your thing as shamelessly as possible.

And soon enough you look exactly like the ridiculous fool you most feared looking like.

Who can take you seriously at this point? No one, thank God—not even you. But that's part of what's liberating about it. Finally, you are not taking yourself so seriously. You are playing, you are out on the dance floor jumping and spinning around like a spastic two-year-old and loving it, and every moment you spend out there wobbling about is a big, wonderful FUCK YOU to the part of you that cares about propriety and appearance and looking cool and all that other crap, to all the dark things in your life and in the universe. You are dancing in response to all that, and it is a good response.

This is why I even believe that dancing to tunes that go against your musical morals—say, for instance, when "Like a Virgin" comes on and you're a man, caught on the dance floor, thinking to yourself, *There's no way I could dance to this, not this song*—is a healthy thing, a blatant act of rebellion against the coolest, stupidest part of yourself. Yes, in the end, there could be nothing better for this group of tight-lipped hipsters than allowing ourselves, even if only for a minute or two, to look a little retarded. "Be the big dork," I've heard Whitey say, testing that out as a motto, and it's a pretty good one when it comes to dancing. Be the fool, have some fucking fun. Embrace the ridiculousness of the act and of yourself and of the night and of life. Shake yourself free from yourself and just dance, not for any reason, really, just because you can't help it anymore, you're having too much fun, and you don't care, finally, what anyone else thinks, you're just dancing, you're just you.

Of course, the other part of me doesn't take too kindly to such rebellion. After all, I have undermined my ego's finely laid plans for myself—all its notions of suaveness and social invisibility—laid them to waste by shaking my ass like a fool in front of everyone, and my ego, disregarded, shrinking like a penis in cold water, doesn't like it. Indeed, the last thing in the world my ego wants is to disappear, it'll do anything to squash my self-rebellion and regain control, and so the motherfucker is screaming at me, louder even than the thumping beats, *EVERYONE'S WATCHING YOU, LOOKING AT YOU WEIRD, STOP DANCING LIKE A DAMN FOOL!* And sometimes this will be enough to jolt me out of the moment back to where I began, all awkward and timid and afraid. But other times it's as if my ego has no chance, I'm above it, I'm too good for such thoughts, I've discovered something more important, this, it, and here I am, I've finally arrived, I've found it! But my ego is a sneaky bastard, it approaches from all angles at all times, and there it already is again, before I even know it—*YES, YOU'VE FOUND IT, YOU'VE GOT IT, YOU'RE THERE, AND DAMN, YOU'RE LOOKING PRETTY MONEY, YOU'RE DANCING LIKE THE BOMB, ALL THE WOMEN ARE CHECKING YOU OUT AND LIKING WHAT THEY SEE, YOU'RE THE FUCK- ING MAN!* Yes, if it doesn't get me one way, sinking me in fear, it gets me the other, swelling me with illusory confi- dence, and then, like some praise-hungry performer, I am dancing for an audience. And then it seems like this is the way it is with the whole room, every move of everyone on the dance floor mechanic, robotic, too planned, a grand act, and I, too, am just one more exhibitionist, dancing to be seen, recognized, swooned over by beautiful girls for whom I and only I could be the answer. Except I don't want this, I want my actions pure, motiveless, their own reward, I want to be dancing just to dance and for no baser reasons, yes, this swell of ego bothers me maybe even more than my fearful self, and so I am trying to ignore it and wrestle it to the ground, yes, again I am battling my ego and wishing it would shut the fuck up, I am cursing myself and my big, stupid human's brain, and this is no way to dance, my ego has succeeded, I'm all caught up in my mind and have lost the beat, and my feet stutter and knees tremble and I am dancing duck-footed and awkward yet again. . . .

Oh, my ego is a remarkable beast! Look how hard it tries! Look how terrified it is of losing control! Look at the lengths it will go for self-sabotage! Yes, like a two-year- old devil-child, some imp of the perverse and pointlessly contradictory, my mind seems to do exactly what I wish it wouldn't, almost entirely *because* I wish it wouldn't. Any- thing to get a rise out of me, to get me reacting, battling, anything to draw me from the sweet refreshing moment back into its labyrinths. . . .

And against such an adolescent foe, there's almost no move you can make. Attempt to shut it out, pretend it's not there, and you invoke an increase in its volume; start arguing with it and you take on a battle that will only escalate. At least that's the way it seems with me—the more I struggle against my madness, the more it rears its ugly head—so that all I can really do in the end is let my mind just do its thing, let its insignificant murmurs rise and fall and remain exactly that: insignificant murmurs. Besides, from the right perspective, that's all they really are, anyway: curious things, comical, extraneous, absurd, and worth at most a mystified shake of my head and a resigned smile. From the right perspective, your ego butting in is worth about as much of your time as the asshole who bumped you as you were making your way to the dance floor—in other words, none.

And so instead of withdrawing back inside to try to wrestle my madness into submission, I go the other direction. I shift my focus to the world around me, to the things that actually matter: the moment, the music, the act of dancing itself. Yes, overcoming that part of me, it can't be an internal thing—some bloody battle fought deep in the caverns of my mind—it's an external thing. It's opening my ears and listening to the beat, it's opening my eyes and having the courage to look up, and take in the night, and be there, and dance. It's making the informed decision to keep on dancing, in spite of and because of it all.

And dancing can kind of solve—or dissolve—everything, if you let it. Because if you truly pay attention to where you are and what you're doing when you dance, there is simply no room for anything else—the act is too all-encompassing. Yes, when you're moving your body to the beat, your hips shifting and feet stepping in time, it's such a physical, visceral act—the music flooding your ears, the bass buzzing in your bones, your muscles twitching and flexing in response—that it keeps you where your feet are. It gets you out of your mind and into your body, into the moment, into this world where you are moving and sweating and beginning to glow, it puts you here on this dance floor where there are all these beautiful people courageously doing their best to be here, too, couples swinging each other warmly around and laughing, beautiful women dancing back to back, or in little oval groups, the hopeful men sauntering themselves casually closer, here where a tall man and a shy pretty girl in a summer dress are dancing together perhaps for the first time, awkwardly, bravely, here where the lights are flashing white and red and purple and blue, and the DJ is up there nodding his earphoned head to the beat and spinning his shit, and it's good shit, this beautiful song is rumbling and shaking all of us to pieces, from wiggling toes on up, disintegrating us, and there's just something miraculous about moments like these, when a fat, funky tune fills the room and everyone in it, even those sitting, can't help but groove at least a little bit—slick-haired cats are tapping their feet underneath their VIP tables and lighting cigarettes to enhance the moment, the models perched above them on the tops of banquettes are throwing their arms in the air and swaying silly with laughter, and they seem like little girls again, a little tall and goofy and awkward, all elbows, but somehow even more beautiful, and everyone is somehow young

and beautiful again, a woman with a broken leg is leaning against the bar and thrusting her crutch in the air, the
old man with the baseball cap is looking down with great
pride and pleasure at the sight of his old feet shuffling to
the beat, Fatdog is chortling like Scooby Doo and swinging
his little friend around like he's about to release her into
orbit, Whitey is doing his wombat boogie with that smile
on his face like he's on Ecstasy at a Dead show, the little
sunshine brunette is doing her giant sweetness bunny-hop,
and somewhere, probably up on the balcony looking down
on it all, even Zoo, who hardly ever dances, is shaking his
thing, pulling his hip-hop boxing moves and swatting aside
invisible midgets—and all these people, all these individuals with their mountainous, anonymous burdens, they are
letting all that shit go and finally having a little fun, they
are dancing and all those long days and lives are behind
them now and now there is only this, this sweet night, and
it is enough.

Yes, this moment is what the night was meant for. Everyone struck by the same beat, united by it, annihilated
by it. The dance floor packed close, alive with movement,
trembling all around you, and you cannot tell who is who
even if you tried, all those writhing bodies and limbs intertwined, all those heads of hair tossed to the beat, all those
hands in the air, and how sweet it feels to finally lose yourself in something bigger, this ancient, communal beast of
the dance. Because we are not so much individuals anymore as we are cells in a giant organism, every one of us
quivering with the vibration of the music, and it is dark but
the air is electric and the lights are flashing on and off and
everyone is no one and we are all simply dancing, anonymous, disappeared, and then maybe they will even release

the mist, the fog machines hissing and the white cloud descending on the room until everyone is sunk in it and you cannot see a thing, just this blank white before you pulsating purple and blue and white with the lights and you cannot see a soul, though you can feel them all around you, the heat of them, and you can hear their howls.

And we have danced ourselves somewhere primitive—when the fog clears, you can see it in the faces around you, sweated through, as if everything extraneous had been burned away, turned to steam and faded with the mists, leaving something raw, animalistic, true. Everyone finally here for once, and yet somehow not here, too: lighter, as if they've left part of themselves behind.

And I've left part of myself behind, too, danced away my ego and all its unnecessaries, arrived here, in the sweet humming madness of the moment. Nothing between me and the world around me. Simply existing, disappeared and found. Yes, if only for a moment, I am just dancing, and I cannot describe how sweet it feels to finally be free of myself and all the rest of it, to be celebrating existence with a grateful stomp just because it's been too long since I did so. For it's at moments like these, when I lose myself, that I somehow stumble across my real self—the ridiculous me with the goofy grin that dances around my apartment in my bathrobe just because life is worth dancing to.

And I will be pulled away, lose myself in myself again—the nature of such beautiful moments is that they are brief. But there are those rare nights when it's as if I have burned through some false, extraneous layer of myself, dead skin, and I emerge from the dance floor scrubbed clean and glowing, my head on straight, priorities in line, alive and awake and in love.

**7**

*The Big Dream: Women in the Night*

> Don't give up, Moe. The girl of your dreams has gotta be in *some* bar.
>
> —HOMER SIMPSON

**AS I EMERGE FROM THE DANCE FLOOR,** the first thing I see is this beautiful woman coming toward me. She is a brunette, and I love brunettes, but this is not what draws my attention to her. What gets me is how different she looks from everyone else. Though there is the crush of the crowd all around her, she is in no hurry. Unlike all the other women who navigate the room with sharp glances and elbows, she seems at this remarkable ease with herself, and with everything else, patiently floating along. She seems above it all, not in any haughty way, just in the simple way she carries herself: She is tall and her slender back is perfectly curved and straight in all the right places, and her long neck with the dark curls tumbling around it, and her face— open, curious, beautiful, looking up. Yes, amongst all these hunched people with their eyes darting down and away, she is the only one looking up, and this somehow makes it seem like she's the only one really there. It's as if she is the full moon and the rest of the room shadowed satellites—I cannot *not* notice her. And I cannot help what happens to me when I do—the way my tired old heart suddenly swells big enough to make the blood burn in my cheeks, the way I am for a moment annihilated, washed almost all away, the only thing remaining an expression of pure wonder. And I am terrified and in love and warm all over and I want to grab her arm, say, "Whoa, wait a second, who *are* you, and just where on earth did you come from?" But before I can do anything—and what exactly I could have done I really don't know—we are forced to pass each other by, pushed by the flow of the crowd in opposite directions, she out toward the dance floor, and me into the room from which she came. And that's how easy it is for a beautiful woman to ruin a man. Just walk on by.

New York is a wonderful and horrible place to be a man. Beautiful creatures are always passing us by. They seem to be everywhere at all times, and gone just as quick, their mere presence and inevitable absence more than enough to drive us mad. Take the city spring, for instance, those first warm days when the women bloom and shed layers and reveal beautiful pale skin and smiles, and they put on short skirts and summer dresses and big sunglasses, and there is style there, and sex, and we see knee and calf and thigh, we see nipples perking out through thin T-shirts and silk blouses, and there is simply no doubt about it: The women are out and strutting it, walking that New York walk, the click of their high heels drifting down the concrete, spinning men's necks. Yes, the spring is a wonderful time to have our hearts broken every few seconds, so devastated by each passing beauty that all our other worries are swept away, leaving on our faces blank looks of idiocy and awe, and men can be seen during this time of year commiserating and shaking our heads as we smoke our post-lunch cigarettes in spots of sunshine, groaning, sighing, cursing, and blessing the spring and its women, in our eyes a look of great distance.

It is not our fault for being so overwhelmed, so annihilated, so utterly undone. New York women, after all, are the world's strongest and grittiest and most beautiful girls, all packed into one towering city. Yes, they are not just women, they are the essence of women: This is *woman*, boiled down into some sort of ideal. Because there is every sweet imaginable kind here, and if they were somehow all combined—which in a sense is what you get, a single blurred vision of a thousand thousand faces passing you by—you would have this archetype, like Plato's chair, this thing that would be all woman and nothing else, an unbelievable feminine presence no man in his right mind could look at without going insane.

Her skin would be brown, firm, Brazilian; her large eyes, set deep and wise and sultry as an Indian princess's, would be a fiery Irish green; her legs would be long, endless, Scandinavian. She would have the shining smile and inner glow of a California surfer girl, the round ass and rhythm and full red lips of an African queen, the breasts, firm and young, of a university first-year. And crowning this goddess, the wild flow of her hair, streaked with blond and red and brown and white and black, as if the light had struck it in shocks at different times of day, the bright morning blond, the hot midday sun frizzling it red, the late afternoon a golden brown, the white of moonlight and deep black of night. A stunning *mezclada*—the face of a beautiful future—she would be everything woman is, and who could handle that? Thank God (yet curse him, too) that this one New York woman is divided into some six or seven million.

But mostly, thank him. Thank God for all the infinite varieties. For those tiny specimens of the female form, five-one tops, beautiful but tough as nails, eyes all spark and sugar. For the too-tall women, big boned and gentle as giants, softness in their movements and curves, breasts that are good for napping. For the husky-voiced girls who are forever rushing about, their lips and eyes and hands quick as little birds, nothing ever enough, always turning their heads and fluttering away. For the ones who do not need to move, whose very presence, still and watchful, emanates that soothing, womanly calm. For the women so stunning their beauty is almost wicked, severe and sharp, mere glances as cold as witches' tits. For the women whose beauty is quieter, warmer—you may not even notice it till you are inches from the kindness in their eyes.

This is New York, and to continue such a list would be an infinite undertaking. Suffice it to say that there is every kind of woman here; suffice it to say that I understand not a one of them. Yes, it hardly matters that that "one woman" has been divided up: Even individually, they're intimidating enough. Every woman has that presence about her, after all, that good old-fashioned feminine mystery, that unnameable something that makes men shake their heads and sigh.

I should admit that women are a mystery to me. The way they are right here, yet somehow distant as far galaxies, and just as unknowable. Yes, for all I know about them, they might as well be an alien species. (Actually, if you think about it, the re-creations of aliens do always seem to have a certain feminine presence to them—those long, thin necks and limbs, those large oval eyes as black as night. They look like models: tall, slender, graceful beings.) And it is of course the impossibly distant differences that I love and am drawn to. All those things they have that we do not, that prove they are such a different breed of creature. Breasts—what the hell are breasts, and why are we so obsessed with them? And the curves of ass and of hips—what god created such sublime lines? "What immortal hand or eye/Could frame thy fearful symmetry?" Yes, Blake, those lines of verse, though they never quite seemed to rhyme, apply to tigers and women alike. Who could have made a creature of such proportions, and why? What is the point of such vicious beauty, if not to torture us with the hope of some final answer embodied within it? How could God have put all that possibility before our eyes, and then make it so impossible to attain?

Oh, but I am not complaining. I guess that's the just way I like them—as terrifyingly beautiful as tigers, their existence as incomprehensible. I guess I like the fact that I cannot get my head around them, that their mere presence can reduce me to the babblings and gurglings of a six-month-old child. Yes, in the end, I guess I just like them scary, deep and dark and mysterious as the night itself.

And that's it, perhaps—women are such the perfect symbol for the night and all its big dreams: that ethereal beauty, out there somewhere in the darkness, waiting for you in flesh and blood. What bigger dream than women? Right there and yet impossibly distant, impossibly different, impossibly impossible. And I love that love is difficult, that it is our answer and dream and does not come easy. It makes you think it must be worth it.

## GODDESS WORSHIP

Truth be known, women are the only reason men like me even go to these ridiculous places, anyway. They are the reason I do this shit to myself, night after night after night. In fact, women might just be the reason I ever do anything at all.

Yes, women are the thing that drives the night as well as the thing it is driving toward—they are the horizon. And it's not even their choice—women are the evening's grand focus, whether they like it or not. Men's eyes are drawn to them, to their glow, to the way they seem to float through and somehow above the crowd, as beautiful and untouchable as ghosts. (Actually, women, too, probably spend more time looking at each other—scowling and judging and comparing—than they do at men.) Yes, the rest of the evening is shadowed, but beautiful women shine. You can see the way the whole night orbits around them, bends and tilts their direction, as if seeking out their light. You can even see men circle them like doomed meteors, their hopeful orbit getting closer and closer, till they almost inevitably break into their atmosphere at the wrong angle and burst into flames. Oh, there's no doubt about it: Women rule the night and, in return, the night bows down to them with a kind of quaking reverence.

It may be an old cliché, equating the feminine with night and moon and darkened hours, but that doesn't mean it isn't true. Unlike the day, a time supposedly ruled by man, and where even in the modern age a woman is somehow still likely to get paid less simply because she's a woman, everything is reversed at night. Here, it is the women who reign. Or as Zoo puts it, "Dude, hot chicks out at night get away with murder." They will wait in no lines, pay no fees.

They are attended to hand and foot; any desire they have, they need merely beckon. Grown men can be seen scurrying away and back, quick as eager little mice, fulfilling their requests. Yes, in the end, the night in New York is indeed a kind of goddess worship—offerings are constantly being made to them of flesh and food and drink.

And all for good reason. The night *needs* women. Their presence can make a time out on the town, their absence can ruin it. This, in the end, seems the very reason door policies were invented, and why it's so hard to get into a club if you're a guy, and so easy if you're a beautiful girl— because when the delicate balance of male and female gets skewed, so does the party. Indeed, one of the few times you will ever see Zoo actually sulk is when there's a paucity of women. "Yo, dude," he will say, glancing around with narrow, sullen eyes, "this shit depresses me, yo. Let's break out." And I feel the same way. When there are no women, there are no possibilities. It's like the night has been drained of its life force, like there's almost just no point.

But when there are beautiful women afoot—especially the tall all-American blondes with sunshine smiles, a little preppy but with a hint of porn star in their eyes—Zoo can be heard saying things like, "God bless beautiful women, dude. They just put me in such a good mood."

And I will say, "Me too, dude," and he will say, "*Mad* prospects, dude," and I will say, "Given, dude, it's all about the possibilities." And we will both stand there with that faraway springtime look in our eyes and that happy warmth in our hearts and drink our drinks, feeling pretty good.

Yes, when women abound, it makes a difference for everyone concerned. Females themselves, sensing safety in numbers the way exotic antelope might, can let loose a little bit, relax into the night, have their own good time doing their own thing without the constant threat of ambush. And the men, well, suddenly all the men are happy, almost goofily so. We are giddy little kids in a candy shop— we hardly even know what to do with ourselves anymore. We are glassy eyed, struck with wonder, overwhelmed to sedation, the beast in us finally soothed.

A man can ask for little more than this, than to be surrounded by the fairer sex. At this point, you almost don't need to do anything anymore. You can kind of just sit back and relax. Sometimes it hardly seems to matter if you hook up with any of them or not, it's just about being around them, this bounty of beautiful women, their soothing presence, their shining calm. It's an odd thing, that some creatures have the power to do this—to soothe you with their mere existence—but it is this way with beautiful women. It's enough to simply know that they are there.

Well, almost enough. Supposedly, I am a man, and I am supposed to *do* something about this. I am supposed to approach one of these mythical, fleet-footed creatures and somehow convince her not to run away.

### THE GREAT GRAVITY OF THE NIGHT

Theoretically, it should be easy. These places are meeting grounds for an exchange of flesh. Yes, the night is where society has dictated we should interact with the opposite sex, flirt, play at love, love, and you can see the way it's all set up for it, the way the whole night seems geared to provide this, to lubricate and smooth the process of man and woman coming together. The alcohol, the dim lighting, the music and the dancing, all those bodies pressed so close together in the heat and thump of the night, all that skin on display. Add in the base biological urge at the root of us—not to mention that theoretical want, too, for love—and the act seems almost inescapable.

It is the great gravity of the night: man and woman hurtling inevitably into each other. You can see it, especially around three in the morning—prime lurking hours—everyone falling into each other, flesh pressed against flesh in corners and at banquettes and on the dance floor and up against the walls outside the bathrooms, everywhere someone hooking up with someone, the happy, bleary, drunken smiles of people in brief love.

And I understand how it happens—I've been there myself—the way, at a certain point of inebriation in the night, you can just kind of fall into someone, and she into you, and then there you are, kissing this girl you've never even met, and you're not even sure how it happened, neither of you probably are. All you know is one second the two of you were innocently dancing, the softness of her pressed up against you and moving to the music, and the next her tongue tasting of vodka was in your mouth. And there's no real deep explanation for it. It was as if the two of you had simply sized each other up with drunken, lusty eyes, recognized the same animal thing there, and that was enough, that you were there, conveniently located. Late at night, it hardly seems to matter who you fall into—you both just want a little physical presence, a touch of that eighth-grade excitement. And that's often all there is to it: Just like in eighth grade, you found out someone liked you, and that was enough to make you like her, too.

Chances are you won't even go home together, and maybe you'll exchange numbers but probably not, probably you'll lose each other in the crowd when she goes to the bathroom, and that was that, just a kiss in the night. And the next day, reminiscing with Zoo, you will be reminded of that moment, and this huge mischievous grin will spread across your face, and you will say, "Oh, *yeah*—I *kissed* that girl last night." It was so natural an act, you'd almost forgotten it had happened. . . .

Of course, the sad fact is sometimes—most of the time— you're one of the ones *not* kissing the girl, the only one in the world, it seems, and that's when you sit there with the great gravity of the night doing its thing all around you, all these men and women drawn together, thinking to yourself, *How the hell can I not be hooking up? I mean, what the fuck—all these monkeys around me have someone—why not me?* And considering how perfectly everything's set up for this consummation, the way the night's whole design urges it on, it really sometimes feels like you'd have to be an idiot to end up alone. I mean, how can you miss?

But then there's the other side of it, and the saving grace for fools like me—despite all the evidence to the contrary, there's a solid argument to be made that nightclubs are in fact horrendous places to find women.

For one thing, there are just too many of them, left and right and all around, all these devastatingly stunning creatures pouting and laughing and sashaying about, and while you might think this a good thing (and it is), it can almost be a version of the sublime, overwhelming, like a lion trying to attack a trillion zebra, no way to single one out.

Even if you do manage to focus in on one, what exactly are you going to say to her, here among the clashing din and bump of the night? Yes, the music's so loud that you have to shout to be heard, though it hardly matters whether they hear you or not because conversations in screams must necessarily cover purely elemental bases, and are hardly worth the effort. Rare indeed is the club conversation between man and woman that goes, "But my idea about the string theory is . . ." More likely you will say your name is Taylor, and she will call you Tim. You will say, trying to be cool, "I can't stand this place," and she will ask, bringing her fingertips to one flushed cheek, "*What's* wrong with my face?" More likely, she won't even let you get that far. Nightclubs, after all, are notorious feeding grounds for carnivores, and so these women are appropriately guarded—experts at ending things before they've even had a chance to begin. No, this is not Brazil, where chicks in bikinis will catfight for your affections, or however the hell it is down there. This is New York, and these girls are tough. They've heard every pickup line ever uttered, and out at night, some of the beautiful ones have gotten it down to such a science that no matter what you ask them, no matter what you say, the answer is no. "Um, excuse me." "No." "Hi, what's your name?" "No." "Didn't we meet at—" "No." "Your skirt's on fire." "No."

No, no, no. And it makes sense. In the night, women are celebrities of a kind, and if they listened to every inane question and comment and pickup line that the hordes of men tossed to them, they'd never make it across the room. Besides, they've heard this shit so many times, the endless variations on the same question, that they have learned what every question a guy asks them really means, and they've simply come up with an appropriate response. "Sex?" "No."

I am a man. My experience is limited. I could never know all the intricacies of the reasons women have for doing the things they do. Or do not do. But I cannot find it in me to blame you, gentle ladies. No, I do not envy you your choices in the night. I mean, look at the men a place like this draws in and deals up, just look at us fucking guys: a bunch of overgrown boys, roughhousing and slapping each other on the back and talking shit and checking you out, making our sly (or not so sly) approaches, offering ourselves up to you in the same old ways again and again and again. It's like one big cock auction, all these meatheads pointing our dicks in your direction. You must be fucking sick of it. It is no wonder that at the tip of your nighttime tongue the word *no* is always waiting.

It is no wonder that sometimes you will not even bother with the word *no,* not even bother with a glance, just let your cold shoulders do the talking and walk on by. And those rare times you do consent to conversation, it is understandable that you will sheath yourselves in makeup and various costumes, that, like superheroes or secret agents, you may even disguise your identities. (Yes, you can never really know if you are talking to the person they say they are, and the only reason I'm aware of this is because I had the amusing fortune of meeting a girl whose fake name was my own true name, and that was how I discovered this whole thing they do, because I was like, "Your name's Taylor? No way! That's my name, too!" And I think she was so taken aback by my genuine enthusiasm that she felt obligated to admit that "Taylor" was in fact only her false name she gives out to guys she doesn't want. "So what's your real name?" She paused and thought for just a moment too long: "Brandene . . .")

Oh, you just keep dishing it out—if it's not a wrong name, it's a wrong number. So it is that the next day, or the day after, or the day after that—or however long it is we're supposed to wait till we can call without scaring you off—we ring the number you gave us and hear on the other end of the line your sweet deception confirmed by a computer's cold recording: *"DOOP, DOOP, DOOOOP: THE NUMBER YOU HAVE REACHED . . . NEVER EXISTED."*

And yeah, it's kind of funny, but it's sad, too, all this camouflage and misinformation and deception, all these defense mechanisms women are forced to resort to. And I do not hold them responsible. Oh, man, it's tough for girls. The shit they have to deal with out at night. The way they can't even have a normal conversation with a guy without that certain sexual tension. The way that some women—and I did not know this till just recently—actually have to think about how to dress so as *not* to get hit on; they can't even have fun and wear the sexy clothes they want, they're too afraid of being a target. The way they have to be so tough, so guarded.

And it's not just the night's annoyances—the moment's groping and general harassment—that women are protecting themselves against. It's all the fucked-up shit that's happened to them in the past. It's history. It's men. It's idiots like me. It's all those times they gave out the right number and the guy never called. It's that one-night stand that left them feeling even emptier than before. It's all the relationships that went awry, all the hurt and the sickness and the shit. . . . And not all the pain and confusion can be claimed by women exclusively. When it comes to sex and love, the past has put us all on guard, men too.

Because we have all wounded and been wounded—we

have all broken hearts and had our own hearts broken and felt the sickening hurt of both—and our skin has simply hardened in response. And the defense mechanisms just feed off each other, an ever-expanding maze of constructed walls, castle gates, distant, guarded, lone towers, and after a while there's just no way to get through. Shit, these days you can hardly even say hello.

And it really is a great tragedy. It shouldn't be like this. It should be simple, casual, as easy as the night would wish it. After all, sex, love, the coming together of two human beings—you can't get more natural than that. But despite this, and despite all the evening's efforts to help us find each other, the final truth is that it's as improbable here as any other place. In the end, it hardly seems to matter that men and women are "meant" to be together—out at night it often feels fucking impossible. Indeed, considering how we're all fucked by karma when it comes to sex and love, it can sometimes seem remarkable that anyone ends up together at all.

## SMOOTH CATS, AND THE REST OF US

What's really remarkable is that some guys make this shit look easy. With only a glance, they can topple castle walls and make the maidens inside forget whole histories of heartbreak. Take Hobbes, my roommate, who, when he was single, was the man. Some men just are. He would do ridiculous things like lean over the bar at some hip New York lounge, look down its length, and just motion a girl over, beckon her with a single stroke of a finger, and she would come. I've seen him do it.

And I don't get it. It's like Zoo at the door. I don't understand where they get the confidence, the conviction, the balls. I mean, where's the intimidation, the fear of rejection, the doubt? Why, for instance, when Hobbes and I are standing at a bar and I say to him, "Wow, she's fucking hot," nodding at a nearby sweet thing with a quaver in my voice, will Hobbes reply, "You want me to introduce you to her?"

"What, you know her?" I'll ask, my heart leaping.

"No," he'll respond, smooth as ice, "but I'll introduce you to her."

I guess some guys have it, and some guys don't. For those of us who don't, there are of course all sorts of theories on how to get it. Take this advice, given to me by a lovely young friend of mine, that the best way to meet a girl these days is to "insult" her. "You can't say the same things every other guy is saying—you have to set yourself apart." Her point was that you can no longer get away with just complimenting a girl like a normal guy would—that instead of bubbling over with praise and mentioning something sweet, yet common, like "I love your dress," you'd actually be far better off saying, in a tone laced with potential sarcasm, and with a skeptical glance up and down her frame, "*That's* an interesting choice for this evening. . . ."

And it might all be true. The days of the gallant gentleman wooing a woman with sweet words have passed. Now, honesty seems the opposite of the best policy—if you like a girl, the last thing in the world you want to do is show it. Instead, there is the constant feigning of indifference. It has become perhaps the most common form of seduction: eyes averted, as if you couldn't give a fuck. It is this way with men and women both, this affectation, but women of course are better at it, more beautiful and graceful, the way they smoke their cigarettes with that gentle arc in their wrists, the butt at the tip of long fingers, exhaling the smoke with a well-blended mixture of dispassion and disdain, as if they were somehow already exhaling tomorrow's failed and ruined dreams. Indeed, so many people out at night practice this art of indifference that, logically, the perfect couple would be the ones who had no yearning for each other at all. As long as they were equally apathetic, it could theoretically last forever—a fully mutual absence of love binding them together.

But the thing is, I do have interest. I fall in love at the drop of an eyelash. I see someone beautiful and bored and it makes my chest hurt. Yes, I'm just no good at appearing to be things I am not: disaffected, dispassionate, icily removed. The fact is I am none of those things. The fact is my heart is swelling, and it shows. It's burning all over my face.

Of course, if it were only that look of awe and love on my face, I wouldn't really mind. At least I would be being myself. The real problem is that there's this feeble attempt at cool smoothed across my features as well. I do not mean to do this. I'd rather be natural. But somehow when I approach a woman, I find myself caught in some sort of mindfucked trip—*I am about to interact with a member of the opposite sex*—and the result is that almost instinctually I attempt that hardened Tom Cruise stare I learned in sixth grade—the narrowed, sex-singed, laser-beam eyes and the cheeks sucked in a little bit, you know, a *look,* steaming sexuality and masculinity. And this look might almost be believable were it not for the fact that there are all these other things streaked across my face, too—my eyes wild and nervous and terrified and in love, my eyebrows arched as if proposing the classic *Night at the Roxbury* question, "You, me?

You, me?" and the awkwardness and intimidation and the blood rushing to my face and all the rest of it—so that the end result is that when I approach a woman, I must look totally deranged, a sex-starved maniac with the goofy-toothed grin of a four-year-old child, and I'm coming right at her. Can I really blame her for turning away?

The sad truth is, part of me is hoping that she *will* turn away so I won't have to deal with actual communication. Because when I speak to a beautiful woman, it's like my heart stops pumping oxygenated blood to my brain—I feel weak-kneed, disoriented, hands and lips trembling—and if they will give me the time, I will (with some luck) stutter and bumble and say stupid things with a quaver in my voice like, "Um, yeah, so, you enjoying yourself this evening?" Sometimes I won't even be able to come up with that ingenious remark. Indeed, there are moments I become so inept in the presence of a pretty lady that not a single goddamn word will come out of my mouth. I mean, here's this amazing creature I know zilch about, and yet inexplicably I will have absolutely nothing to say or ask. It's like every sensible thought in my mind is snuffed silent, like I'm strangled by her beauty and cannot breathe, like if I opened my mouth and attempted to speak, the only sound that would emerge would be a kind of gurgle of a question that a dehydrated ostrich might emit—"Ghheulkk?" There have been numerous occasions when, unable to breach the awful awkwardness, I have simply smiled, nodded in polite terror, turned around, and walked away.

Knowing that I might fail so miserably at even the most basic small talk makes the notion of approaching a girl fill me with so much dread that I hardly do it anymore, unless I'm egged on by my friends, and even then I usually only make it about halfway there. Indeed, this has become one of my signature maneuvers: to approach some beautiful thing, and then, struck by terror just before I reach her, to whirl around and flee in the opposite direction.

And so it goes tonight. When I return upstairs to our perch where the crew is chilling, Zoo stops me in my tracks before I can even take a seat: "Dude, check it, man"—he points behind me with a big mischievous grin—"Natalie Pibbly, dude. Go talk to her."

I turn and there she is, just a few strides away, Natalie Portman, whom I have loved since it was probably illegal, and suddenly, all my composure and hard-won battles are gone and I am timid as a frightened little kitten again. But I muster as much courage as I can, and I do it, with this huge stupid grin on my face I am doing it, it's really happening, I am walking up to say hello to Natalie Portman!

But I have chosen a bad moment—her back is turned and she is talking to someone else—and not wanting to interrupt her, I stand there awkward for a moment, and then that moment becomes an excruciating two, and I am close enough to reach out and touch her shoulder but instead my hands are nailed to my hips and, struck with terror and indecision, I do a 180 and retreat to the couch, where Zoo is shaking his head and laughing his ass off, and so are all the other guys: "Get back over there, you monkey."

And so, muttering curses at Zoo and the rest of those bastards sitting there contentedly on their stupid couch, I make my way back over to her, finally tapping her on the shoulder and saying, breathless and as fast as my tongue will go, "Sorry to bother you, I just wanted to say . . ."

And she is very sweet. She does not turn away, there is no gut-reaction "no," and there is no obvious disgust in her eyes, either. She does not really seem bothered to be bothered by me—she seems interested, even, and I'm sure I'm grinning like an idiot and stuttering, but she is very calm and sweet and beautiful, terrifyingly so, and my heart is big and swelling and I am warm all over and I am thinking, *This could be it.*

But she is leaving, her coat is folded over a slender arm. And this is the way it goes, out at night and in life. Beautiful things are always disappearing. . . .

And there is nothing you can do about it.


## THE ART OF NON-SEDUCTION

And so I say good-bye to Natalie Pibbly and let her drift off into the evening, and return reluctantly to the jackals at my table.

"Dude, what happened, man? How could you let her go? What the fuck?"

"She was leaving, dude, what do you want me to do?"

"Something, man, something."

But there is nothing I could have done, not really. Sure, maybe I could have been more of a dick. Maybe I could have said, "Queen Amidala, that was a good role for you, real solid performance," with a flicker of disgust in my eyes. But I didn't. That's just not me. (And it probably wouldn't have been Nat Pibbs, either. She seemed too cool a cat to be impressed with such cock-faced nonsense.)

And the truth is I'm glad I'm not that guy. Because, yeah, I admit it—I'm no good at playing the game, but I'm not so sure I'd really want to be, even if it did get me more ass. The way it's all conducted these days, I don't know. Everything's gotten too complicated. All those roles we're supposed to play and things we're supposed to do. Procreation has become politics, full of murky symbols and secret handshakes and gestures that look like they mean one thing but mean other things entirely. Nothing is on the surface anymore—if it ever was—nothing how it seems. And I've gotten to a point in my nightlife where I just don't have it in me.

Not to say that being on the hunt and playing the game can't be fun. It can. It was. All those nights out with the boys, women our only goal, conniving and elbowing each other and picking out prospects from the shadows and whispering, "Look at those legs, dude: so trim."

"Dude, if she kicked you she'd break a rib."

"She could punt a football like a hundred yards, dude. . . . Go get her, man."

"No way, dude, she's way too absurd. She's like Wonder Woman or some shit. You go get her."

"Dream, dude."

All the false bravado and shit-talking, all those nervous approaches and rejections, all those emotions rushing through your veins and your heart thumping in your face, and oh, man, all those nights of seeking—I do not regret them—but it was the search itself, the feeling of a good buddy and you on the hunt, united by purpose, prowling one club and the next, all that possibility out there—and not the infrequent, happenstance "successes"—that I will remember fondly. (Besides, a lot of the time, not even success is necessarily success. Take a look at Fatdog, for instance, whose little brunette friend has been clinging to him throughout most the evening in a rather Ewokian manner. When she gets up to go to the bathroom, he leans over to me and whispers, "She likes me. It's terrible.")

No, none of those pursuits ever led me where I wanted to go, not really. Indeed, when I think about it, I'm not even sure I've ever "picked up" a woman in the night. Oh, I guess I do okay when it comes to the fairer sex—I've had my occasional flings or girlfriends—but the majority of the time it happens, I'm either introduced through friends or it's that kind of random, inevitable, drunken falling-together I described before. I've never actually hunted one down, as far as I can remember. When I end up with a woman, it seems an act of grace. Yes, the term "getting lucky" has kind of lost all meaning, but that's what it seems when it happens for me: I get lucky—with undeserved good fortune, I bumble upon them clumsily. Or perhaps it is they that stumble across me, see something in me—what, I have no idea. It's certainly nothing I'm doing on my part, as far as I know. . . . (Actually, I seem to end up with women almost exactly *when* I'm doing nothing on my part—and I think there may be something to this.)

After all, the strange truth is that to actively pursue the fairer sex might work against you, in the end. A woman can sense a man on the hunt, get a whiff of his predator scent, and be scared off. Yes, I've spent enough time scurrying after them, scraping and digging, to have learned that women do not react well to such overeager, squirrel-like motions. They pull away from arms that reach. They do not want the man on a desperate search for them; they do not want a man with too much want in his eyes. This is the way it is with all human beings. It's engrained in us to lean toward the things that shy away, and retreat from the things that advance. And this is part of the reason that the art of seduction is such a delicate matter, because you are seeking something that resists being sought.

And so to make women the sole focus of your night, your mission and only contentment, you're already way off-course. In fact, you're taking a path that somehow leads away from its own destination. After all, what brings two people together at first, this is mystery, this is scent and fate and other impossible things, and you cannot seek out such moments, they will come or they will not. Love will happen, or it will not, and any concerted effort or action on your part will most likely only make it less likely. So it is that you are left in a rather absurd dilemma when it comes to women in the night: There is nothing you can do, not really. You can neither act nor not act, speak nor not speak, and any which way you're screwed.

It is a strange feeling—to be in love and want with all these women, and know that there is nothing you can really do about it—but it is not a bad one. I'm all good, right now, sitting here with Zoo and the boys, my dream girl gone into the night, another lovely thing vanished from my life—and, sure, there is a part of me that is heartbroken, but I am okay with that, I am okay with that rush of ruin in my chest. It makes me feel alive, somehow.

Besides, Natalie Portman? I mean, come on. How could I ever have expected that one to work out? She was bound not to happen, bound to leave—she really was a dream—and this is the way it always seems with love in the night. What we want is forever something we do not have, something we probably could never have, some impossible, perfect fantasy, more specter than flesh. Yes, this is the night—a thousand trillion dream girls appearing and disappearing before our eyes—and there's something strangely beautiful about it. I constantly feel as if I am waving from a ship bound to some far-off battle. You look so lovely standing across the growing water, out of earshot, fading into the distance. It is heartbreak out here, and I love it. (In fact, I do not consider it a good night out unless my heart has been broken at least three times.)

That is the night, that is life—this endless longing for things just out of your reach—and it can be pleasant at times to exist consciously in this spot, to be so close to your desire you can smell it, almost taste it, and yet at the same time to know that you are somehow separate from it, above it, okay without it. To know that you are your own man, under your own control—content, confident, having your own good time in spite of and because of it all.

Yes, strange as it may sound, it *feels good* to have lost Nat Pibbs, to have had my greatest fantasy release me from its hold. It's liberating, somehow. And sure, now that Natalie Portman has vanished into the night, I guess I could be up and chasing down the next dream, but I'm glad I'm not. It feels good to not have to, to be fine where I am, free for just a moment from this frantic search for women. It feels good to make the decision that all the nonsense and drama is not worth your time, that there are more important things to focus your attention on.

Because this is life, this moment, and you are out with good friends and the music is bumping and you still have that flush of energy from dancing, you still know what's important, and it is this that is important, not some unattainable dream but this, this moment of celebration and of living, this always too-short night. And to tear yourself away from this moment, from being happy as you are, to play all those games, get wrapped up in all the nonsense and heartbreak and loss, and in the end, to pursue something that retreats when you pursue it, well, it just doesn't make any sense. At this point, a drama-filled girl looking your direction, it's like being offered crack—you kind of almost just have to laugh at the offer. (Of course, the ironic thing is, this is when women actually *will* start looking your direction.)

So when Zoo starts jabbing me with his elbow and nodding across the way and saying, "Dude, those chicks are checking you out, man, hook it, dude," I have little choice but to reply:

"*You* hook it, dude."

"Dude, dream, man, it's all you, dude. I got a girl already."

But I am shaking my head and grinning and saying, "Nah, dude, fuck it, man, it's not worth it. . . ." And Zoo and the other guys are looking at me like I'm crazy, but I feel like I'm the only sane one.

So when the two cute girls across the way get tired of making eyes at me and getting no response, and they wander off into the crowd, I let them go. The night is almost over. There is no time to waste. Indeed, it is nearing last call, and Zoo and I have decided to go to the bar for a final round of shots.


## MURPHY'S LAW OF LOVE

"Tap! Zoo! What's up?" Zoo and I turn from ordering our shots of chilled scotch to discover our old friend Doc, who grew up with Whitey and Fatdog out in the Long Island summers, there from out of nowhere at our side.

"Hey, man, what's up? What the hell are you doing here?" Doc is an unlikely candidate to be in such a place at such an hour. He's a country kid at heart, and has spent a lot of his life in the mountains—his music bluegrass and not this thump-thump-thump shit.

"Yeah, I had some friends in from out west, wanted to show them a good time. Which reminds me, hey, I want you guys to meet E."

And I don't know how I hadn't noticed her, but there she is, standing right behind Doc, the apparition I saw when I was coming off the dance floor, the one with the posture and eyes and curly dark hair, the one with that shine. We all exchange hellos and handshakes and Zoo and I order more chilled Dewar's shots so that everyone can have one, and when the drinks arrive, she downs hers like a pro, doesn't even bother with the ice-water chaser. "Not bad," she says, which no one but Zoo ever says.

We get along well from the start. Everything's natural, somehow, easy, and as such, it's not long before I mention to her, idiotically, how I noticed her before—"I don't know, you just looked different from everyone else. You were, like, actually looking around and stuff."

She laughs and says, "It's probably because I'm from out of town."

She's from Colorado, and is here in the city to visit Doc with a group of girls, including, I think, her sister. She tells me that back home she is a yoga teacher and massage therapist. I tell her I find that impressive. "Why?" she asks, a touch suspiciously.

"Because if you're gonna be healing other people, you kinda have to have your own shit together first."

She laughs. "That's a good answer," she says.

And she does have her shit together. She is right there. Her eyes are open and deep and dark and honest and looking right at you; you can see in them something flashing and awake, something real, as if the thin veil of fear that clouds so many people's eyes has been burned through, leaving just her, just this curious, beautiful being staring out at you. And there is nothing sharp or intimidating or cruel about her beauty, either. Instead, there is only that glow, that soothing womanly calm.

And of course she's just a girl—a fucked-up human being like the rest of us—and I'm sure she has her own issues and walls and I'm sure she's been hurt, too, in the past, and hurt other people as well, but still there seems something not hidden about her, something natural, something true. The strange thing is, you are feeling this way, too. Like you have nothing to hide, either—not anymore. Like you've burned through your own haze, sweated out your pretenses and your darkness, your desires and deceptions and illusions, like you are done with all that, beyond it. Like finally and for once you are simply yourself.

And so instead of all your usual neuroses and fearful bumblings, it's surprisingly easy to talk to her—you're not stuttering or spitting on her or anything—you're actually interacting with her like a semi-normal human being, and your heart, though warmer and bigger than usual, is in your chest and not your throat. In the end, you even manage to say a few things that make her laugh, and when she does she puts a calm hand on your arm and you get warm all over, and you are thinking, *This is it. . . .*

Of course, this is not it. She is from Colorado, after all, and it turns out that tomorrow she will be leaving. Back to her mountains and trees and rivers and sky. And this is the way it goes, out at night, and in life. The ones you fall for are somehow always leaving. If she is not from Colorado, she is from Lebanon, London, Australia. She is leaving to-morrow, the next day, a week later for Los Angeles. And, once again, there is nothing you can do about it.

And of course that's the way it happens—that when you finally give up on finding a good woman, she appears. And that when you finally think you've found her, she slips away.

Who knows why it's like this—maybe it's just Murphy's Law of Love in the Night: always fucking you, one way or the next. Maybe this is just the way the night perpetuates itself, always almost giving you what you're looking for, but never quite.

I guess it would be easy to get depressed about the whole thing. To be one of those dejected, crestfallen faces in the corners who cannot for the life of them seem to find what they are looking for, but somehow I am not. Somehow I'm okay with the fact it could never really happen. After all, maybe the reason I fall for impossibilities is that there's a strange part of me that does not want to find something possible. Yes, maybe the truth is that I don't want an end to this particular search—maybe I just want the looking, maybe I just want the want. Maybe I have fallen in love with the night as it is—full of dreams that were never meant to be realized, that were only ever meant to be dreams.

Of course, in the moment, with this beautiful bodhi-sattva before my eyes, I'm not actually thinking about any of this stuff. In the moment I just know that it's all exactly as it should be. The fact that yet again I have ended up fall-ing for a woman who will be here for this one and only night—I don't know, it's fitting, somehow. Yes, though I cannot say exactly why, I am filled with a strange certainty that tonight is perfect as it is, that it couldn't be any other way. And so instead of being sullen or dejected, I am wide-eyed, awake, in love. Yes, though it makes no sense, I am in love—with the grand absurdity and hopelessness of it all, with the moment and with life and with this beautiful creature before my eyes.

Because in the end, it doesn't matter that she will disappear—all that matters is that she is here right now, and so am I, and the night is not over yet. All that matters right now is this. And this warm moment of brief, impossible love, it is enough. It is more than enough.

"What are you smiling at?" she asks. She is smiling, too.

"I don't know," you say. "Nothing," you say. . . . "Everything." You want to hug her, or kiss her, or tackle her, or something. But instead you just stand there grinning like an idiot.

"Where's the bathroom?" she asks.

"Come on, I'll show you," you tell her, and you take her hand and lead her through the crowd.

# 8

## *Morning Comes*

Have you seen the snow leopard? No! Isn't that wonderful?

—PETER MATTHIESSEN

**EVERY NOW AND THEN,** as the night winds down, I find myself looking out over the remains of the scene in a quiet kind of awe. Though it is late and friends have drifted off and the crowd has thinned, the party is somehow going stronger than ever—the music is still bumping and everyone left is still stomping and laughing and carrying on— and, I don't know, there's something about the spirit of these people, nearing four in the morning, still digging in. It's an amazing sight, all these human beings gathered here in the darkness, still celebrating in spite of the ungodly hour and all the rest of it. It is important, somehow.

And maybe what makes the whole scene so beautiful now is that you know it cannot last. You can feel the night slipping away, right before your eyes. And not just this night, but all nights. Because there's something in the way that any given night draws to its close that reminds you of all those other nights that did the same, of all those other good times already lost, and it is easy at such moments to feel as if everything is ending.

And it is. I know this sometimes, with complete certainty, and it breaks my heart. My time out here—my nightlife—I feel sometimes like it's nearly gone.

"We're getting a little old, Zoo," I remind him at times like these, when it occurs to me.

"Yo, fuck that, man," is his emphatic response. "You know we still rock it like we're eighteen."

And we do. Here we still are, after all, nearing four in the morning, the party still rocking and so are we. But the simple fact is, whether we act like it or not, we're not eighteen anymore. We're ten years older at least, pushing thirty, and the majority of the people out here are far younger than us now. They're where we were five, ten years back, their faces are fresh and strange and unfamiliar, and the old familiar faces just keep getting fewer and farther between.

I don't know. Maybe I've had my time out here. Because there used to be the feeling that this was my world, my moment. But not so much anymore. That sweet sensation of being young and out in the night—of infinite possibility, of things about to happen, of the night and life all ahead of you—all of that is behind me. The night belongs to someone else now, to the young. It is forever their place, their time. And whether Zoo chooses to deny it or not, he and I and all the rest of our crew really are getting a little old. I don't know how much more this life of the night has to offer. It is perhaps nearing time for me to move on to something else. . . .

And I really have been feeling this recently: separate, aside, on the outside looking in. Though I do my best to participate, to get out there in the middle of the madness and dance myself fresh-faced again, I am becoming an on-looker, and maybe this is why, more and more these nights, I catch myself staring wistfully out over the crowd the way a father might watch his children at play—with a strange mix of pride and nostalgia. I am happy to see that even when I'm gone, the night will not end, that there will be others to dance in my footsteps. But I am sad to have to go.

And this sadness I feel when I pause toward the end of the evening and breathe it all in, it isn't just for all the nights that have ended already, for all those good times already lost—and for the fact that that was me out there, not so long ago. Yes, the weird thing is that I am feeling nostalgic for a thing I haven't even lost yet. For the night that surrounds me right here and now. Because even as I stand here experiencing it, I can feel it slipping away, lost and found at once, like a beautiful woman passing you by. And it is a strange sensation—to feel like I am losing something that is right before my eyes—but it is not necessarily an unhappy one. It makes you realize, if only for the briefest instant, that nostalgia is forever attached to the moment at hand, that this is it, the thing you will be longing for in the future, the times you will look back on with that ache and pang and sweet sting of remembrance. After all, here you are, at the place you want to be, surrounded by the people you love, and for a moment—who knows what does it, if it's just neurons induced to fire by that last shot of scotch, or the strangely familiar perfume of the girl who just passed you by (a scent that reminds you of the first girl you ever loved), or if it's the fact that it is late now and they have just slowed the music, thrown on an old-school Talking Heads tune (*"And you may ask yourself, well, how did I get here?"*)—the simple fact is your heart is swelling, and you know that a moment like this cannot last and so it is beautiful and so you are in love, and so you feel good. You are finally happy—if "happy" is the word—because you are sad, too. All you really know is that here you are in this beautiful place, this beautiful time, and you do not want it to end.

## THE NIGHT BEGINS AGAIN

Here in New York, no one ever wants a good night to end. But whether we like it or not, the night is always ending. The arrow of time moves in only one direction, after all, and the nights make you feel this most sharply. Always too brief, too swift, these evenings are over before they've even begun. I mean, when you take away all that time spent getting places as opposed to being there, you have what, maybe two or three good hours out here in the thick of things, maybe less? So if it has been a good night, it is always over too soon.

This is partly why the lights always seem to come on far too early, even though in reality it is far too late. When they cut the music and flick the switch, there is a collective groan of sorts—even now, 4:15 in the morning, no one is ready for the end, not yet—and people can be seen shielding their eyes and squinting up at the cruel glare in disbelief. There is this moment of bewilderment, all these faces everywhere, stunned and blinking in the bright.

And it's a blinding new world, now that we can see. Gone are everyone's comfortable little circles, hemmed in by shadow and recognition; the room has opened up, become three-dimensional, full of distances and gaps and barren walls, and everything is big and bright and ugly—you can see the sludge on the floor, the stains on the couches—and you can see all the people now, too, a whole ballroom's worth of faces, and in the sudden light, everyone, even your friends, look like strangers.

Except there's something familiar about these faces, too, at this moment, even the ones you've never seen. Yes, you can look at almost anyone at this hour and recognize them, understand exactly where the other person is because you're there yourself. You've each made it here, all the way through the big night to this absurd moment, and somehow you all feel the same unlikely way about it: It happened too soon. Strangers look at each other and commiserate, grinning and shaking their heads—*It's too damn early for it to be this damn late.* Yes, we've been through the same shit, after all, all of us, and here we still are, past four in the morning, the survivors of some epic battle, the battered final few, still standing, still wanting more. And you can see it. Behind the fatigue there is something fresh about our eyes, almost as if we'd been worn so thin there's nothing left to hide the glow.

Yes, we've been up going on twenty-four hours, but sleep seems the last thing on our minds. And it's not even due to the drugs. It's something else. An energy in the air, in the night, in us. As if just being out here, doing our thing, taking in the night, it's like drinking some elixir. It feeds, nourishes. So that at the night's end, you are buzzing with it, every cell of you is humming. We look more awake now than we did when the night began. We look satisfied and hungry. We do not look like we are about to leave. We look like we are about to arrive.

We gather our things in the mean brightness and head for the sweet relief of the darkened city streets.

And things can be so clear when you walk out of the madness into the predawn city night, your ears still ringing with the absence of the music, the relative silence of the streets. You feel like you have just stumbled out of some epic concert, haggard but somehow scrubbed fresh. Where before there were only bodies everywhere and heat and madness, suddenly there is the cool, sweet early-morning air, there is space, and up above the buildings, sky. You look around at your friends, at the other people spilling out of the club into real life again, and it is on them all, this disorientation, the foggy emergence from the nightclub world into this one, everyone as if just waking up, their eyes blinking and their smiles disbelieving—*Is this even possible? Am I really even here?* Except it is a pleasant disorientation, the world is tilted and so are you and nothing is quite as it was before the night began. It has brought you somewhere. These same streets no longer look the same. Everything is sparkling, crystal, the air is fresh, you are lighting up cigarettes in the predawn cracked blue twilight and marveling at the new universe around you, taking it all in. And whole civilizations bloom outside these clubs at this hour— Middle Eastern men are grilling beef and chicken and lamb for kabobs, hot-dog stands compete, there is the line of yellow cabs, the limos there, too, and the men selling individually wrapped roses, two for five dollars, that only suckers like me ever buy, and the little guys in hoods passing out colorful flyers for parties tomorrow night and the next that end up scattered across the pavement like autumn leaves because no one cares about tomorrow night because tonight isn't over yet. And it isn't. There remains this crazy, senseless energy in the air—sure, there are those who slither drunken into cabs to mutter their address and

pass out for the ride home—but the majority of us who
have made it to this hour somehow have more in us. We
are still looking for something to do, we are planning big
things, coordinating after-parties and rounding up straggling friends and pretty girls and checking our phones and
hooting across the restless crowd to familiar faces on the
other side. And the night is about to begin again.

You must think we're crazy, to want to go on to another
party at this hour, and maybe we are. Maybe it's a sickness,
not wanting the night to end. But I cannot help myself. I
feel this urgent need to see the night through, till every
moment of it has been explored, every possibility juiced,
every shadow illuminated. (Not everyone is like this. Other
people, when it gets late, something in them starts to tick—
*gotta get home, gotta get home, gotta get home*—and if the club
closes or the dawn begins to crack, they will flitter like bats
back to their shade-drawn bedroom caverns.) For me, it is
different. I love the morning light. Seeing the sun come up
means the night has gone on just long enough.

Besides, how could we let it all end now? We've been
moving toward this place all night long, dancing and grooving ourselves here, and now that we've almost arrived, it's
over? It doesn't seem fair. I mean, I just found my girl, my
groove, my nightlife. Things are finally coming together.
As Zoo is fond of saying at this abominable hour, *Things are
just getting started.*

But even when everything doesn't fall into place just
right, I still won't let the night end. Yes, even when it
makes no sense—when the hotspot has closed and all my
other friends, even Zoo, have already gone home—there's
a chance I will head off on my own to one of the mega-
clubs that remain open after four though they no longer

serve booze, and I will drink Cokes and bottles of water and smoke doobies and cigarettes and dance solo on the giant darkened dance floor with the lasers and the steam and the thumping beats and the thousand strangers dancing all around me—all of us still trying to get to that place, or there already, finally just dancing, annihilated, alive— until I will emerge alone, 8:40 in the morning, bone-tired but happy, into a morning sun so bright it's like walking into the light at the end of the tunnel when you die.

No one else I know would ever do this—head off on their own to dance solo in a giant club till the sun is good and up and not an inkling of the night remains. I guess something in me simply urges me on.

Sometimes, I would stay up forever, if I could.

Because there's more out there, more to be found—and even if there's not, it feels like there is—and it would be criminal to turn my back on it, on all those possibilities. And so even when it makes no sense, I like to see the sun come up. I think it has something to do with not wanting to miss anything.

Yes, I think that's it, the reason I cannot stand going home until there seems no other option: Something might happen in this final stretch of the night, and I cannot bear to miss it.


## PERFECT ENDINGS

In the end, all that time you spent clubbing tends to blend into itself; all the thousand discos and lounges and bars and nights become one indiscriminate place and time, one long, crazy blur. Ironically, it is the late-nights you might just remember. After all, it is often when you leave the club, out into the last shreds of the evening, that things get good and weird.

Yes, this is the strangest time of day—neither morning nor night—and in this inverse twilight, anything can happen, and does. This is the hour when urban legends come to life, when people might black out and end up waking up several days later in Canada, Mexico, France. This is the hour of orgies and lost kidneys, Korean hookers and road trips to Atlantic City, strange revelations and unlikely buddhas. You could end up building a fort out of couch cushions with a buxom blonde, waterskiing at dawn in your underwear, driving your car through a hedge and abandoning it there on some stranger's lawn. There's just no telling what will happen now, and perhaps that is the point. After all, the whole night has been leading up to this moment, building to a crescendo—something is bound to occur, and it could be anything: sex, death, even love.

And it is of course love that you are still hoping for in the end, even at this hour, illogical as it may seem. Yes, even after all the madness and confusion and drama and your informed decisions not to bother, it remains this, even the faintest possibility of it, that keeps you out in the most ungodly of hours and beyond into morning: the chance to hold someone beautiful and warm against your skin, and feel happy. Even now you are hoping to find some kind of answer.

And it's not all empty hope. There are times that the night actually ends the way you so wish it would. Ideally, with some sweet creature in your arms. Maybe you're at an old friend's late-night, and you bump into this girl you have met before but somehow now it's different, you look at each other and each see something new there, something possible, and you talk and laugh and then there you are, dancing with this slender, frail-bodied, big-hearted thing in your buddy's living room, and somehow despite all your neuroses (and the fact you are the only two actually dancing to the music), it's not even a little awkward: You are holding each other and laughing and swinging each other about, circling away and then coming in close, the warmth of your middles pressed together, your lips and eyes inches apart, until it all becomes too intense and you giggle like giddy teenagers and pull away. And when you step out on the balcony to get a breath of fresh morning air, you somehow lose her, think you've lost her forever, that she's disappeared, as beautiful things tend to do, but you keep looking, and finally you find her, curled up in one of the guest bedrooms, and she looks up with sleepy, happy eyes and a big smile and says, "You *found* me," and you have.

Or maybe it is the end of a late-night pool party out on Long Island, and you are kissing this beautiful, freckled creature you met only just that night (but had somehow known forever). And now the party is over and it is just the two of you left and you are in the pool house on the bed and outside it is dawn and morning light is everywhere and the pool is still, and inside, above you, she is taking off her shirt to reveal small perfect breasts the color of pale morning and, circling one hip bone, a crescent-shaped scar she is needlessly ashamed of. And her long strawberry curls are tumbling all around you, and you do not have sex, but you do not need to, this is enough, more than enough, and you are in new, clean, trembling love at this moment, or something like it, and there is nowhere in the universe you would rather be.

But the truth is that these perfect endings are indeed the rare ones. More likely, for instance, than finding your love, you will *almost* find her. Like this stunning Greek named Helen whom you meet at a random after-party and fall for right on the spot—her quick little hands and hips and the way she uses them to emphasize her quick, husky English, her tumble of black curls and face that could launch a thousand ships—before she informs you, tenderly, because she can see you didn't know, that she's an escort. And before you can tell her you don't care and would love her anyway, she tells you it could never work: *Either you're jealous,* she explains, *or you're not—which makes you a pimp.* (You imagine for a brief moment what life might be like as a pimp— wearing a cape and a cool hat, corralling hoes, carrying a cane with a sword in it, bitch-slapping delinquent johns— and decide that as alluring as it might sound [and despite the fact that, oddly enough, you do have a cape and a cane with a sword in it], you just don't have it in you.)

Or maybe you find yourself sunbathing with two half-naked girls at high noon, no sleep going on thirty hours, following the October Indian-summer sun from rooftop to rooftop to avoid the cool shadows, hoping to God you might have a chance at a threesome, but you don't. No, instead of hot three-way sex with two nubile college girls, what will happen instead is that the three of you will wind up standing on the edge of the roof peering down at the Avenue of the Americas, talking about how no one looks up in this city, how no one down there scurrying along knew that if only they lifted their heads they would see near-naked girls looking down at them from a rooftop—"You have to caw," you explain, "to draw their attention. Then I bet they'll see you." "Caw?" "Yeah, you know—caw—like a bird." And so one of them, the voluptuous redhead, steps up to the edge and lets out the most pathetic, timid bird call ever uttered—kind of a "c-caw?"—more of a tentative question than a statement meant to turn heads, and you start laughing. The redhead in her bra and panties tries again, and her slender brunette friend joins her. Again the caws are feeble, and the absurdity of the situation—these girls in their underwear making timid bird sounds over the edge of a rooftop—doubles you over with tears in your eyes. "*You* caw," the redhead says, daring you to do better, so you step up to the edge and let out a powerful, "CAW!" the way it's supposed to be done—after all, you've had lots of practice cawing amongst your friends—and people across the street hear it—such an out-of-place sound reverberating among the concrete canyons—and their heads angle up, they toss ears and eyes to the four corners of the sky, but still they do not see us standing there looking down at them in our underwear. "Do it again," the redhead says, excited now. You let out a couple more clear, powerful, "CA-CAWS!" which have the same effect—everyone down there seems to hear it, you can see the ripple of tilting heads, but no one sees us. No one knows about this but us. And this is how it can feel, when you have been up all night and it is day again—like you and whoever is still up with you are in on this kind of secret. . . .

Or maybe you end up in the penthouse of some random older art-dealer guy, an acquaintance of acquaintances of some friend of yours, and there's absolutely no chance you're hooking up at this spot: The only thing the women here are interested in is the cocaine on the kitchen counter and the hairy-shouldered European men in the hot tub. And so you are sitting at the dining-room table rolling a spliff and debating the state of the universe with a drug dealer who has the gall to say he doesn't believe a word you're saying, doesn't even believe you believe it, wants you to dig deeper, right down to the truth of it—he looks at you with these honest, almost angry eyes and says, *Tell me something true,* and you cannot do it, you cannot think of a single thing to say that you know is really true, and you cannot tell if the man with the eight balls in his pocket and the model on his lap is trying to fuck with you or awaken you, or both.

Sometimes, even the after-party fails, and finding a woman becomes the least of your concerns. In fact, the only two people who show up at your apartment for the late-night are some strange Eastern European girl and, consequently, her muscle-bound, gold-chain-wearing "friend"/cousin/pimp/lover, so that in the end it's just you, sitting across from this random Ukrainian "couple," passing them spliffs and shots of chilled vodka and doing your very best to just be yourself despite the fear you've suddenly developed that they may or may not want to take your kidney. And perhaps it is this, in the end—your basic decision to trust in them completely—that saves you: They see you're just a normal guy, and that you've opened up your home to them happily in spite of the risks, and so perhaps what they are saying to each other in Russian is, *Nah, he seems like a pretty good kid—let's steal someone else's organs. . . .*

Or maybe there will be no girls at all. Maybe instead of some bumping late-night party packed with starved models, food is your final destination. Yes, chow is always a strong possibility, especially if you roll with a consistently hungry cat like Zoo, and so you will spend the last moments of your night with the same monkeys you began it with, your good buddies, giggling and eating chicken wings and cheese fries in ubiquitous New York diners, Papaya King chili dogs on street corners, steak frites and French onion soups at late-night bistros, fish pancakes and grilled meat rolled up in lettuce at random empty Korean barbecue joints, every meal a feast of epic proportions—*The best chow I've ever had, dude.*

The plain reality is, most of these nights will have no perfect ending—all the girls will have drifted off, taking with them that ancient ideal of finding your happiness embodied in warm flesh—and instead it will be just you and the boys. But these are the kids you've lived this life with— you've been through nights like this before with them and here you are again, at the warm, easy end of another perfectly imperfect night out on the town—and so the circumstances hardly matter. Yes, you have battled through the monstrosity of the night together and somehow made it to the other side, and so at this point you hardly give a shit where you find yourselves—you're happy any which way. Maybe you'll all end up in the wreck of your apartment after an all-night Halloween party, rum punch and fake blood smeared on the walls, tattered angels' wings and devils' pitchforks strewn across the floor as if there'd been some epic war between heaven and hell here, but right now the only battle raging is a friendly one between you and your good buddies, full of side bets and finagling, as you try your drunken damnedest to bowl a tennis ball down the muck–filled hallway and knock down the ten empty beer cans set up there like pins. . . . Or maybe you'll all end up at an old friend's house in the early Long Island morning, all the women gone (or at least the ones you would have wanted), no real prospects left, and all your other prospects are looking pretty shoddy, too (in the end, for instance, you will undoubtedly be sleeping alone on your friend's musty carpet with your blazer as a blanket). Yes, nothing has turned out the way you would have wanted it to: There's no more herb, cigarettes are running low, you're sitting at the breakfast table playing Trivial Pursuit for shots of warm rum. And you turn to a good buddy and, shaking your head in a kind of disbelief, ask him, "What the fuck are we doing still up?" but you pose the query with this crazy senseless grin on your face that is somehow the very answer, and he responds much the same, shaking his head and grinning and uttering that old wise statement: "I don't know, man, I don't know." And neither do you. Yes, you don't know anything anymore, you've given up, given in, and you are laughing like a fool at the absurdity of the morning coming in through the sliding screen door, stepping out into a blustery end-of-summer day on Long Island, clouds rushing across the sky and wind and rain and the fall and winter before you, and you feel it all against your skin and breathe it in, and though it is nine in the morning and you've been up all night and are drunk and all the girls are gone and nothing worked out, there is just this clarity there, this strange perfection, a beautiful, rainy end-of-summer day. You feel somehow more awake, more happy, more yourself, than you have ever been. And you grin at nothing, at this failure of a night and the beautiful morning it brought you, and walk back inside.

And yeah, sure, you'd expect the greatest nights to be the ones when you get everything you thought you were looking for, and you end up with a pretty girl in your arms—and don't get me wrong, they can be—but sometimes the not-getting can feel even better. Yes, sometimes the best nights are the ones that fail you, somehow. When you battle through the great stretch of the night, spurred on by all that hope and yearning and expectation, only to come out on the other side and find . . . nothing. No woman, no answer, no enlightenment, nothing. And yet it's just as it should be. You have arrived, if only because there's no place else to go. Yes, you've reached that final point where there is nothing left to look for—no next, no future, no horizon, only this. All those desires and dreams that drove you through the night are gone now, vanished, no more. You're all dreamed out, and it's liberating, somehow. Yes, the night has led you nowhere, really, given you nothing, failed you yet again, and though it makes no sense, you are grinning—at yourself for having done this whole ridiculous thing once again, at the grand absurdity of the night and of the search and of life and of it all—and it feels wonderful. For a moment you are in on the great secret, the oldest joke—that it's all been some grand illusion, some strange, sweet dream—and now that it is morning and the long night is done, you can finally and fully awake.

### TONIGHT ENDS

And tonight, well, tonight ends like most nights do. We emerge from the club, gather our troops, pile into cabs and limos, and head to the after-party. Our destination is Fatdog's parents' place—they must be out of town—and a whole bunch of us are going, Zoo and Stibbs and Whitey and Hobbes, Doc and the Colorado girl and her friends, some other random cats. (Zoo, hungry as usual and craving Korean BBQ, is hesitant at first, but it doesn't take much to convince him: "You think he has any chow there, dude?" "Given, dude." "All right, I'm in.")

When we arrive, Fatty takes over the living-room stereo and sends hip-hop beats bumping through the big apartment into the ears of everyone scattered throughout it—Zoo and Stibbs and Hobbes in the kitchen, attacking the refrigerator, planning big things with eggs and bacon and toast; the girls from out of town in the TV room, looking at the wall of family pictures: Fatdog as a little puppy skiing in the same Colorado mountains where these girls were raised. And me, I can hear the music even in the laundry room, where my beautiful brunette Colorado girl and I have been sent to choose a bottle of wine. But it is nice in there, quiet and close, the music in the distance and laughter, too, and we chat for a while and laugh and she lifts herself up and sits on the dryer, and I stand there before her with my hands on the knees of her thin jeans, looking up at her and wondering if I'm supposed to kiss her. I am, I do, and she kisses me back, and it is the sweetest thing for a moment, much more than I could ask from any night, and all warm inside and grinning like a fool, I pull away and say, bashfully, "I wasn't sure if you wanted me to." And she smiles and hops down from the dryer into my arms and we kiss again for a moment, and then she grabs a bottle of wine in one hand and my hand in the other and says, "Come on, let's go dance. I love this song."

It is a good song, some old funky rap song that reminds me of my first nights out, so long ago, and in the living room everyone is dancing and jumping around. The Colorado girl and I dance well together, too, as I remember it, no awkwardness there, only sweetness and silliness and good fun, though I do notice that she doesn't want me to get too close. Maybe she doesn't want her friends to know what has happened.

And we both know it could never really work. That tomorrow she will go back to her mountains and massages, her yoga and big sky, and that I will stay here in New York, here with my whatever it is I have here. We do not exchange numbers. When we leave Fatdog's, it is a bright and fresh spring morning out, and there is a motion to go to Coney Island. But Colorado is ready to go home, and for once, so am I.

## HEADING HOME

I wish I could tell you I end up with the girl—that we go back to my place in the early morning, have wild sex, fall in love, and are currently living happily in the mountains of Colorado raising little bodhisattvas—but that's just not the way it happens. No, tonight ends the way most nights do—in the end, you go home alone.

It is for this reason, among many, that at the conclusion of every night out, a certain number of young, hopeful human beings head home disappointed. You can see it in their stride—not much of a stride at all, more of a whimper of a walk, dejected—they may even angrily kick at proverbial pebbles if they appear in the path of their boots. Whatever they were looking for they did not find. No love for them this night, no happiness, no answers, no nothing. And I understand this. Back in the day, I used to end many nights in similar funks. Maybe it was that I put so much hope into every night holding some sort of meaning, that when nothing came, it was like I had been cheated by

God. But not so much anymore. It's different now, some-how. These nights, even if I find nothing—and sometimes especially if I find nothing—I go home happy anyway.

And sure, there's a side of me that wants not only this night, but all nights, to go on forever—but there's another part of me that enjoys heading home, especially if it has been a long, full night, and I am aware that there is noth-ing left to be found. There's something about the simple act of it, ending the long night's journey with the walk or drive home through the pale, peaceful morning. It can be especially wonderful out on Long Island, driving home at 6:15 A.M. on a Sunday, the sun up but no one else on the roads except for the animals. Birds and squirrels have taken over the pavement, hopping around out there and chatting amongst themselves, deer stand off to the side in the early sunlight and quietly watch you pass, and know-ing all this, you drive cautiously. You have nowhere to go but home now, and are in no hurry. And so it is easy to find yourself almost deliberately missing a turn and ending up at some strange dead-end inlet, where the sun will be cracking open the horizon and burning through the mists; you may even get out of your car just to stand there for a moment in the morning stillness and feel the rising sun on your face.

Back in the big city, these early mornings can be shrouded in a kind of quiet, too—the idling garbage trucks sound like crickets, the swoosh of distant cars like the murmur of the sea. You can hear the twitter and rustle and hop of little birds in the trees planted in the cement, and even the pigeons manage a certain kind of majesty at this hour, soaring and swooping through the light-dusted morning air, all wings and proud chests, their scaly red feet tucked up into their feathers and forgotten. Yes, even here in the concrete jungle, this seems the animals' time, and yours. No one else is really up yet, and those who are up are not awake like you, they are sleepily sweeping the front of their shops or smoking cigarettes and sipping coffee in spots of sunshine—it is perhaps a Sunday morning, a sacred time, and you can feel it in the sweet air, the quiet hush of the sleeping city—and you, you are walking the morning streets in your dark night clothes, feeling very raw and certain and true, and though you are the one who has not slept, you feel like you are the only person awake in the world, the only one alive. You are alone in the world and nothing has been gained, and yet there's something that feels so right about it, so perfect, as if it had all somehow been necessary, the whole night and your whole life essential, and you know it. . . .

It is always good to walk a little ways in the beautiful, forgotten morning, and remember.

## Acknowledgments

This book would not have been possible without the support and kindness of the following people, and is therefore, at heart, as much their creation as my own. First, I'd like to thank my agent, Ryan Fischer-Harbage, the only guy in the business who really got what I was going for, and who was willing to go out on a limb to help me get there. I'd also like to thank my talented editor, Vanessa Mobley, for doing an extraordinary job under extraordinary circumstances, as well as Jenna Ciongoli and everyone else at Random House, for their hard work and boundless enthusiasm. . . .

I'd like to express my deepest appreciation to my family for continuing to believe in me even when it probably made more sense not to, as well as to Lizzy Eggers, whose patience, love, and support helped me make it to the finish line. . . .

Last but not least, I'd like to thank all of my friends—Zoo, Hobbes, Fatdog, Stibbs, G, Benny, Tako, Big M, Whitey, and the rest of you crazy bastards—for making my life in the night just so much fun. . . .

TAYLOR PLIMPTON is a freelance writer and editor based in New York City. His writing has appeared in numerous publications, including *Men's Journal* magazine, *Dan's Papers,* the *Harvard Advocate,* and TheRumpus.net. He is the co-editor of *The Dreaded Feast: Writers on Enduring the Holidays,* an anthology of dark holiday humor published in October 2009. He graduated with a degree in English from Reed College.